W9-CFF-529

Exploring
with
Pattern Blocks

by

Vincent J. Altamuro & Sandra Pryor Clarkson

Cuisenaire Company of America, Inc.

New Rochelle, New York

Cover design by Arthur Caledonia

Copyright© 1989 by
Cuisenaire Company of America, Inc.
12 Church Street, Box D, New Rochelle, New York 10802

All rights reserved
Printed in the United States of America
ISBN 0-938587-09-9

Permission is granted for limited reproduction of pages from this book for classroom use.

Table of Contents

Introduction

Today's world will assuredly not be the one our students will inhabit in the twenty-first century. Skills learned today may become obsolete. As teachers we need to prepare students to function in this unfamiliar environment. Therefore, we need to help our children think for themselves and creatively solve the problems they will confront.

The NCTM's, *Agenda for Action*, recommended that problem solving be the focus of school mathematics for the 1980's. The Commission on Standards for School Mathematics has recently drafted a set of standards concerning mathematics education for the 1990's and the twenty-first century. It states that, "Problem situations should form the context for learning and doing mathematics in grades 5 — 8."[1] Standard No. 1 focuses on mathematics as problem solving.

> In grades 5 — 8, the mathematics curriculum should include numerous and varied experiences with problem solving as a method of inquiry and application so that students can:
> - Use problem solving approaches to investigate and understand mathematical content
> - Formulate problems from situations in the mathematical world and in the real world
> - Develop and apply a variety of strategies to solve one-step, multi-step, and non-routine problems
> - Verify and interpret results with respect to the original problem situation
> - Generalize solutions and strategies to new problem situations
> - Acquire confidence in using mathematics meaningfully.[2]

If problem solving is the primary goal of mathematics instruction, then effective instruction must present interesting, challenging and meaningful problems. "Many problems should be modeled concretely."[3] The authors concur with the NCTM's emphasis on concrete situations as a focus throughout these grades.

Exploring with Pattern Blocks (Grades 4 — 8) is designed to help develop concretely many problem-solving skills. By using pattern blocks in this problem-solving format, students are introduced to, and develop skill in utilizing strategies such as guess and check, looking for a pattern, using logical thinking, drawing a picture, making a list, using a table, and modeling.

The book is divided into five chapters: Explore and Discover, Number, Geometry, Measurement, and Application. Most of the activities can be investigated individually, cooperatively in groups, or as a whole class. On each page, the problem situations are followed by Explore More activities that may or may not be used by the entire class. These may provide needed further exploration or a more challenging extension for individual students. They are investigations you might want some pupils to consider as an additional application or as reinforcement of a particular strategy.

We suggest that the Explore and Discover section be used first to acquaint your students with pattern blocks and familiarize them with concepts that will be developed more thoroughly in subsequent chapters. The activities in each chapter are presented in increasing difficulty, but all need not be tried in sequence. The strands of number, geometry, and measurement can be used in any order, as best they meet the curriculum of your mathematics program. However, before commencing the application section, it's suggested that some of the related challenges in the previous chapters be experienced.

We hope that your students will not only learn from these problem situations, but also learn that mathematics can be fun. Your comments are greatly appreciated. We look forward to hearing from you.

Vincent J. Altamuro
Sandra Pryor Clarkson

---

[1]National Council of Teachers of Mathematics, *Curriculum and Evaluation for School Mathematics*. (October, 1987), p. 51.
[2]Ibid., p. 54.
[3]Ibid., p. 55.

STARTIME

Stars of the same size have been drawn. Cover three of the stars with the pattern blocks indicated. Cover the fourth star any way you want. How many blocks did you use for your star?

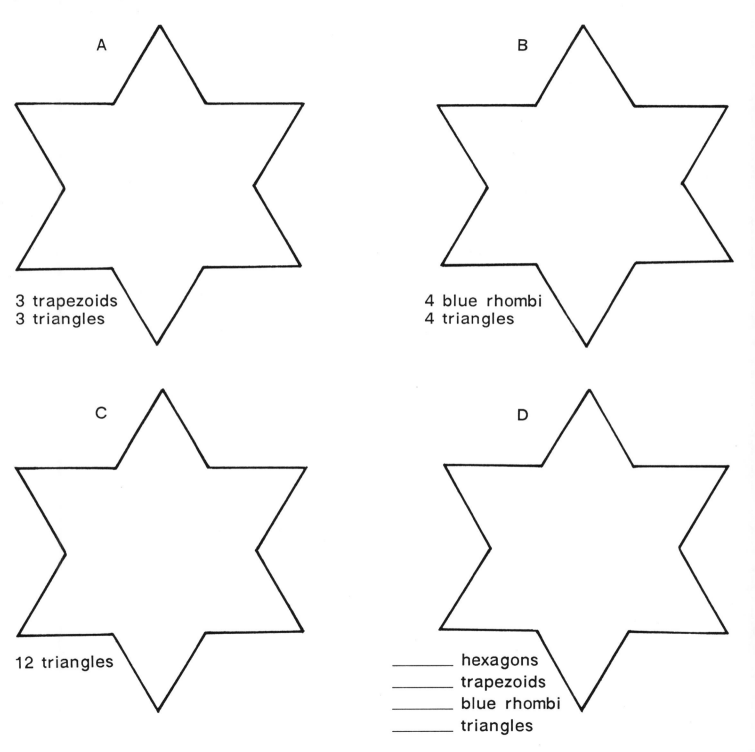

A

3 trapezoids
3 triangles

B

4 blue rhombi
4 triangles

C

12 triangles

D

_____ hexagons
_____ trapezoids
_____ blue rhombi
_____ triangles

EXPLORE MORE: Which star used the fewest number of triangles? The most? Why does the number of triangles used vary? Can you make a star without any triangles?

Exploring with Pattern Blocks © 1989 Cuisenaire Company of America, Inc.

GRETLES

This is a Gretle. Cover it with pattern blocks.

Remove your blocks.

- A. Cover the Gretle using only hexagons. Can it be done?
- B. Cover it using only trapezoids. Can it be done?
- C. Cover it using only blue rhombi. Can it be done?
- D. Cover it using only triangles. Can it be done?

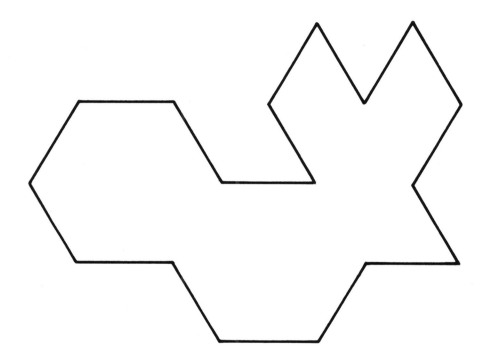

EXPLORE MORE: Create a Gretle that can be covered with only trapezoids. Trace it. Can you cover it with only triangles? Why? Can you cover it with only blue rhombi? Why? Change your Gretle, if necessary, so that it can be covered completely with only trapezoids <u>and</u> then with only blue rhombi.

COVER THREE
(An Activity for 2)

Materials: One cube labeled green, green, red, red, blue, and blue; red, green, and blue pattern blocks; gameboard below.

Directions: Player 1 tosses the color cube, selects the block that has the color indicated on the cube, and places it on any of his 3 hexagons. Player 2 then tosses the cube, selects the appropriate block, and places it on any of his 3 hexagons. Players continue to take turns. The first player to cover all 3 hexagons exactly is the winner. If a player cannot use the piece indicated, the player loses a turn.

PLAYER 1

PLAYER 2

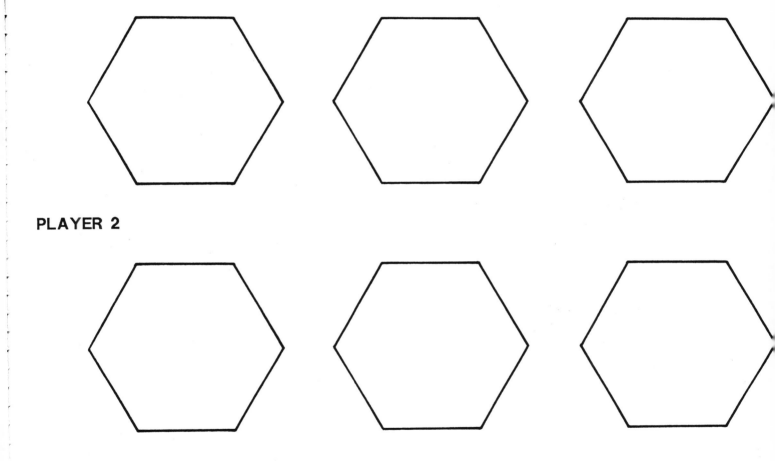

EXPLORE MORE: Each player covers one hexagon using only triangles, one using only blue rhombi, and one using only trapezoids. Play the game as above but this time remove what is indicated on the cube. Trades are allowed. The first player with no pieces left is the winner.

COUNTDOWN 10, 9, 8, ..., 1!

Select the pattern blocks needed to make one of the designs below. Study the picture and count from 10 to 1. When you reach one, turn the page over and make the design from memory. Pick another design and try it again!

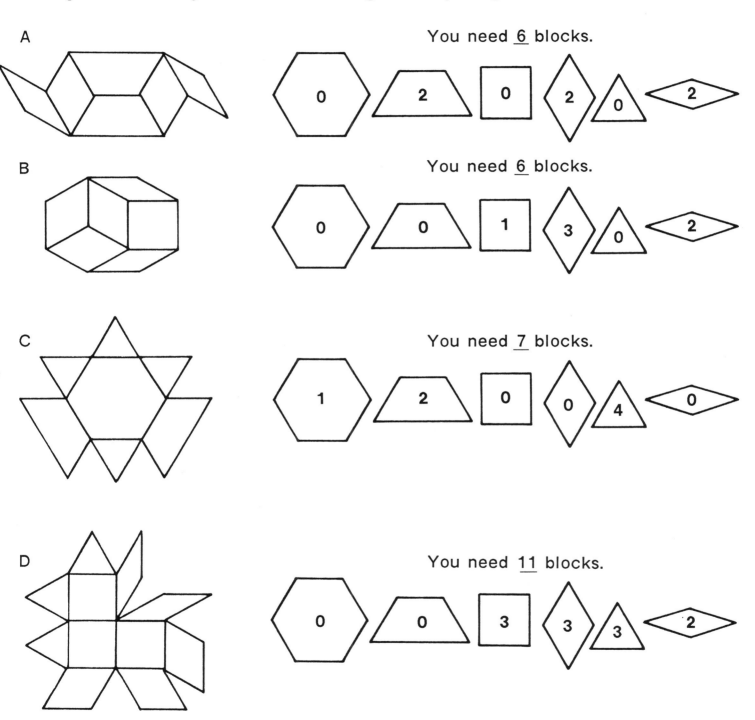

A   You need <u>6</u> blocks.

B   You need <u>6</u> blocks.

C   You need <u>7</u> blocks.

D   You need <u>11</u> blocks.

EXPLORE MORE: Which designs were easiest to remember? Which part of the design did you make first? Why? Try to make them again counting from 5 to 1.

Exploring with Pattern Blocks © 1989 Cuisenaire Company of America, Inc.

SPACE STATION
(An Activity for 2)

Materials: Red, yellow, blue, and green pattern blocks

Directions: Player 1 takes a block and places it anywhere on the Space Station so that it covers one or more triangles completely. Player 2 selects a block and does the same. Players continue to take turns until no more blocks can be placed on the Space Station. The player who places the last block on the Space Station is the loser.

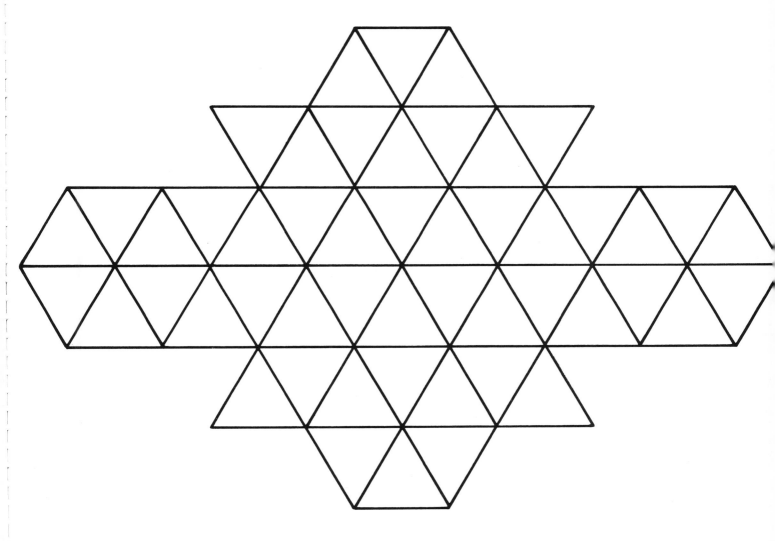

EXPLORE MORE: Change the rules.
1. Play as above but the player who places the last block on the Space Station is the winner.
2. Play as above using only red, blue, and green blocks.

Exploring with Pattern Blocks © 1989 Cuisenaire Company of America, Inc.

HEXING HEXAGONS

Cover each hexagon in the tower a different way. In each hexagon, you may use the same color blocks or you may mix them. Record in Tower A. Remove the blocks and cover each hexagon again in as many new ways as possible. Record in Tower B.

TOWER A   TOWER B

EXPLORE MORE: How many different ways did you find altogether? Do you think you have found them all? Why?

Exploring with Pattern Blocks © 1989 Cuisenaire Company of America, Inc.

TAKE 4

Cover each design using only 4 pattern blocks. Can you find another way using only 4 blocks? Record your findings in figures A and B.

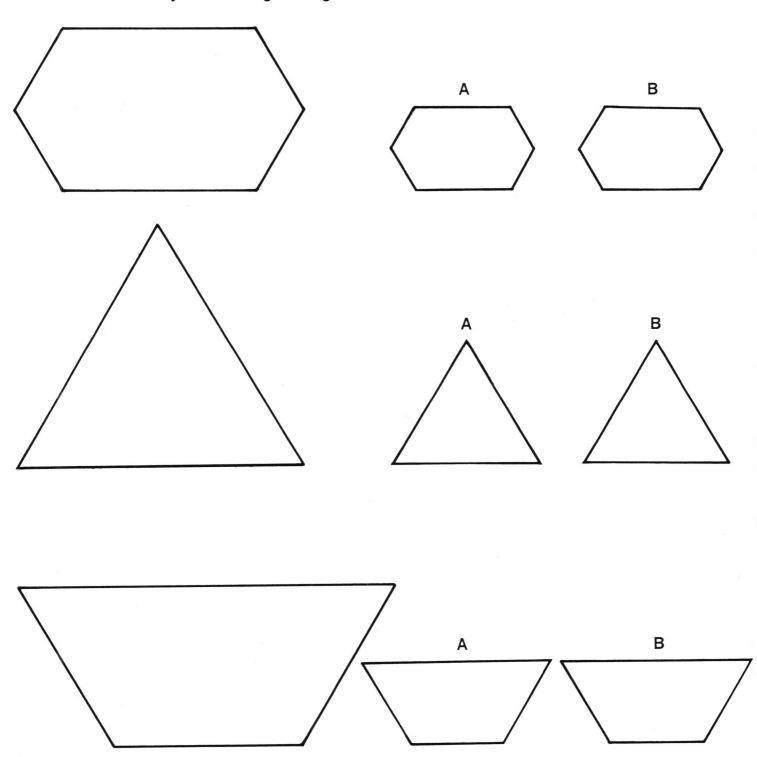

EXPLORE MORE: Is it possible to use more than 4 blocks for each design? Is it possible to use fewer than 4 blocks? What's the difference between the greatest number of blocks and the fewest number of blocks needed for each design?

Exploring with Pattern Blocks © 1989 Cuisenaire Company of America, Inc.

TAKE 6

Cover each design using only 6 pattern blocks. Can you find another way using only 6 blocks? Record your findings in figures A and B.

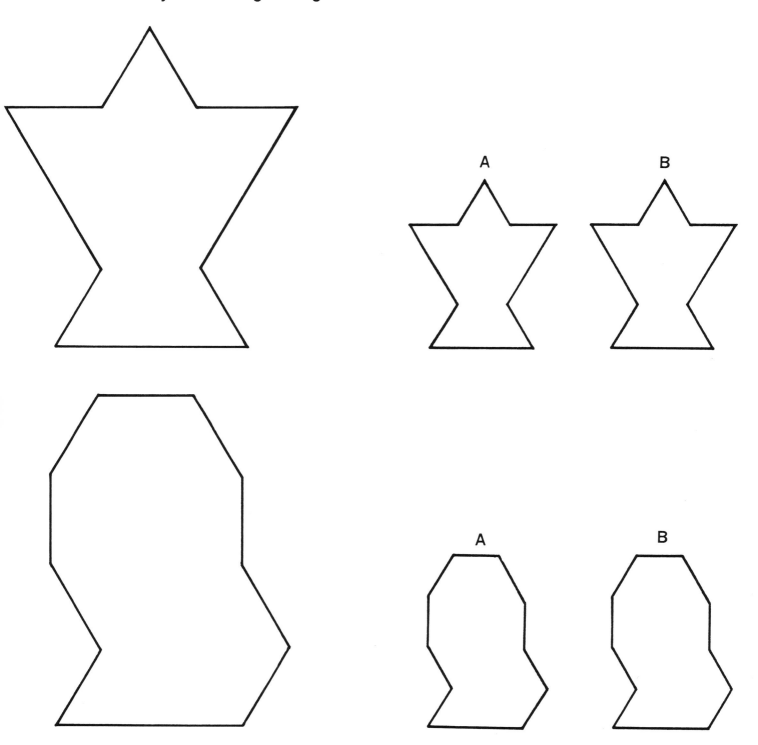

EXPLORE MORE: Is it possible to use more than 6 blocks for each design? Is it possible to use fewer than 6 blocks? What's the difference between the greatest number of blocks and the fewest number of blocks needed for each design?

Exploring with Pattern Blocks © 1989 Cuisenaire Company of America, Inc.

ONE-COLOR DESIGNS

For each design, select one of the indicated pattern blocks. Guess and record the number of blocks needed to completely cover the design. Use the blocks to find the actual number. Do the same for the other pattern block. Complete the chart and compare your results. What patterns do you see, if any?

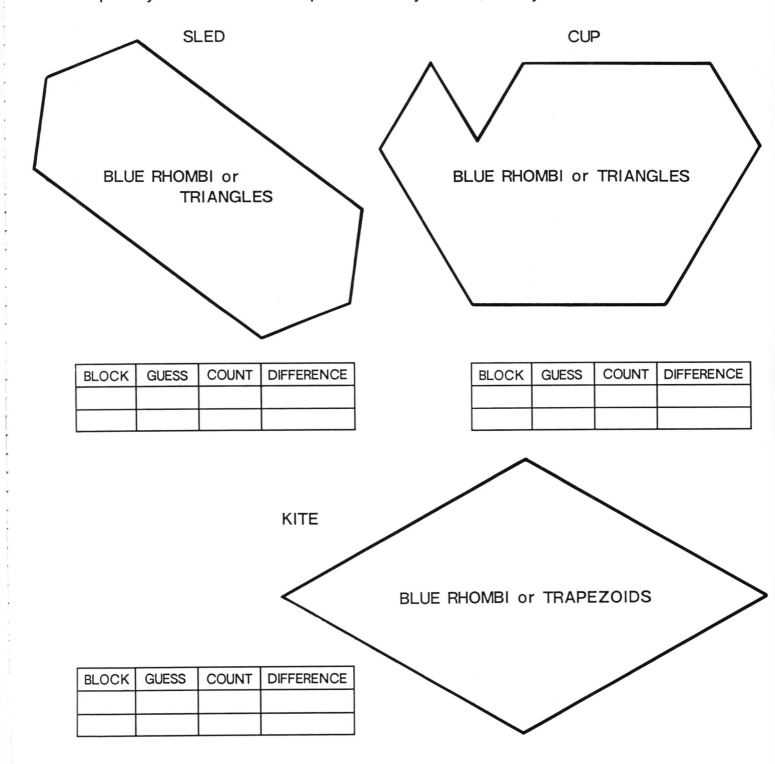

SLED

BLUE RHOMBI or TRIANGLES

CUP

BLUE RHOMBI or TRIANGLES

BLOCK	GUESS	COUNT	DIFFERENCE

BLOCK	GUESS	COUNT	DIFFERENCE

KITE

BLUE RHOMBI or TRAPEZOIDS

BLOCK	GUESS	COUNT	DIFFERENCE

EXPLORE MORE: How many triangles do you need to cover the kite? How do you know?

Exploring with Pattern Blocks © 1989 Cuisenaire Company of America, Inc.

SPACES ZERO
(An Activity for 2)

Materials: One cube labeled red, green, blue, blue and green, red and blue, yellow and green; red, green, blue, and yellow pattern blocks; one polyhedra die.

Directions: Players take turns. On a turn, a player tosses the color cube and the polyhedra die. The color or colors that appear indicate which pattern blocks to select. The number that appears suggests how many blocks of each color are needed to cover the figure leaving no spaces. Before taking any blocks, the player must decide if greater, fewer, or the exact number of blocks indicated by the die will cover the entire figure. The player then indicates the number of blocks he/she thinks are needed and places them on the figure.

Object: To be the first player to reach 10 points.

Scoring: 2 points for correctly guessing the amount (greater, fewer or exact) of blocks needed.
2 points for guessing the exact number of blocks needed.

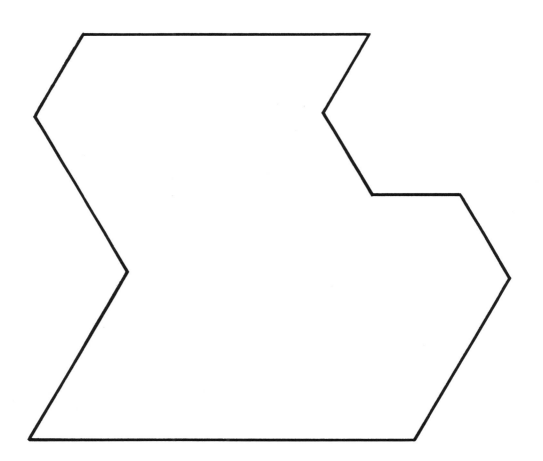

EXPLORE MORE: Using only red and yellow blocks, cover the figure above completely. What is the greatest number of yellow blocks that can be used?

Exploring with Pattern Blocks © 1989 Cuisenaire Company of America, Inc.

SPACE CREATURES

These space creatures change slightly as they move through space. Use pattern blocks to show how they should look in column D. Record what you've built.

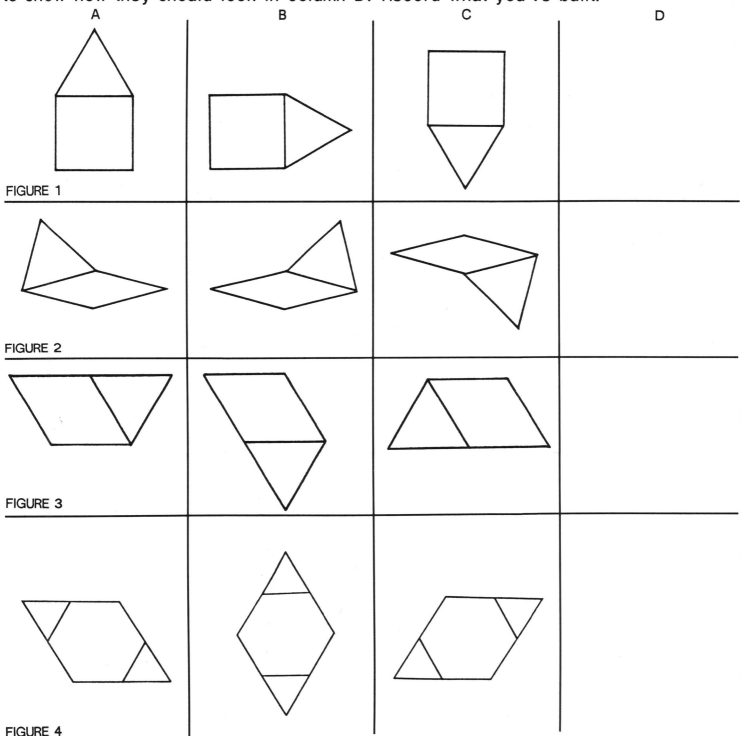

EXPLORE MORE: How many changes are necessary <u>before</u> each creature looks the way it does in column A? How does each creature look after 6 changes? After 8 changes? Create a space creature and show it in three positions. Ask someone to show the fourth position.

Exploring with Pattern Blocks © 1989 Cuisenaire Company of America, Inc.

ASTEROIDS

Create the asteroids labeled figure A. Each asteroid is moving in space. Rotate each one according to the pictures given. What would the next picture look like? Draw it in the space provided.

FIGURE A

FIGURE A

FIGURE A

FIGURE A

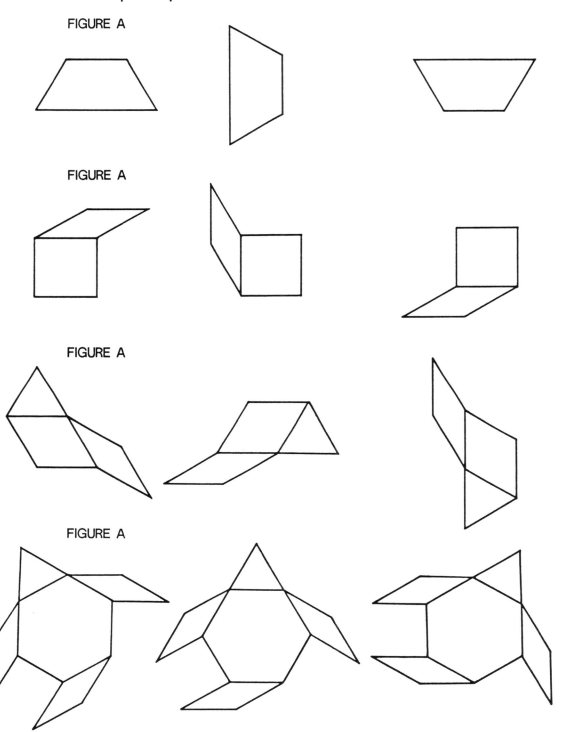

EXPLORE MORE: Photographs are being taken at 30-second intervals. How much time must elapse before each asteroid is back in its original position? Create an asteroid that returns to its original position in 3 minutes; in 1½ minutes.

FOURSOMES

Select the pattern blocks indicated. The pattern blocks in the fence have something in common; the others do not. Determine what the pattern blocks in the fence have in common and decide on a label for the group. Explain why you chose your label.

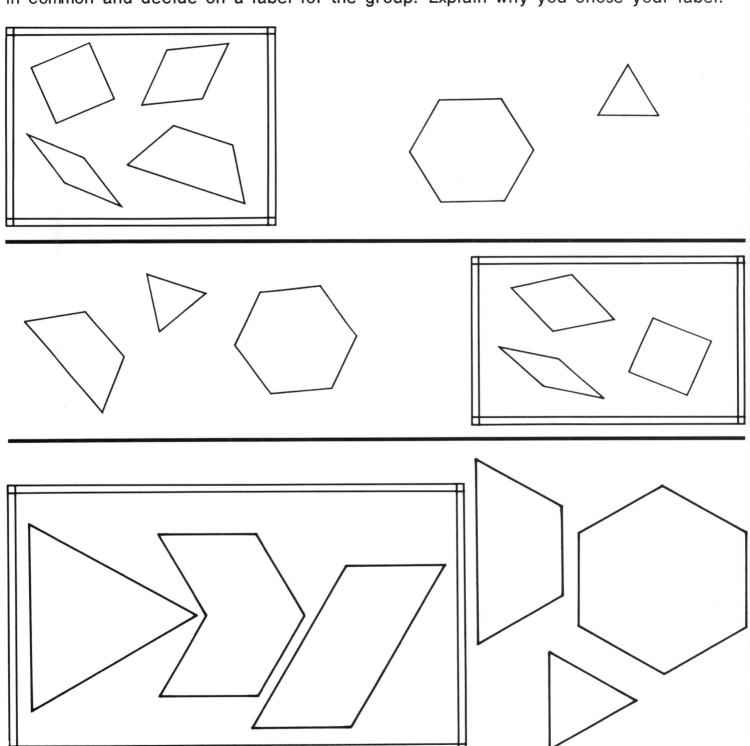

EXPLORE MORE: Place a group of pattern blocks in a fence according to your own idea. Ask someone to guess why you did not include the rest of the pattern blocks.

Exploring with Pattern Blocks © 1989 Cuisenaire Company of America, Inc.

MORE HEXAGONS OR TRIANGLES

Six triangles make a hexagon. How many triangles do you need for 2 hexagons?
3 hexagons? 5 hexagons? Complete the table below.

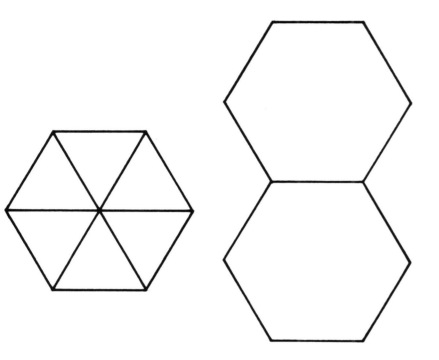

Number of hexagons	Number of triangles
1	6
2	12
3	
4	
5	
6	
7	
8	
9	
10	

How many triangles would you need to make 50 hexagons? 100 hexagons?
199 hexagons? Try to write a rule for any number of hexagons.

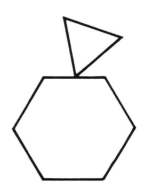

EXPLORE MORE: Using only triangles, make the apple
shown. How many triangles do you need? Make a table
showing how many triangles are needed to make 1
apple, 2 apples, 3 apples, ..., 10 apples. Predict how
many triangles are needed for 100 apples; for 199
apples. Why do you think so?

Exploring with Pattern Blocks © 1989 Cuisenaire Company of America, Inc.

CREATING STARS

Using 4 blue rhombi, form a star like the one shown. How many triangles would you need to make a congruent star? How many blue rhombi would you need to make 2 stars? 5 stars? How many triangles would you need to make 2 stars? 5 stars? Complete the table.

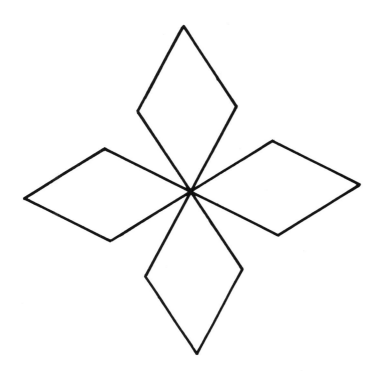

Number of stars	Number of blue rhombi	Number of triangles
1	4	8
2		
3		
4		
5		
6		
7		
8		
9		
10		

How many blue rhombi would you need to make 50 stars? 49 stars? 200 stars? How many triangles would you need to make 50 stars? 49 stars? 200 stars? Why?

EXPLORE MORE: Make a bridge as shown. How many trapezoids did you use? How many triangles could form a congruent figure? Make a table like the one above, indicating how many trapezoids and how many triangles are needed to make 1 bridge, 2 bridges, 3 bridges, ..., 10 bridges; to make 1,000 bridges; to make 999 bridges.

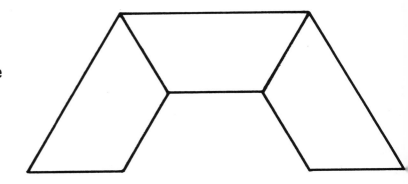

GRAB BAG MYSTERY

Suppose, without looking, you put your hand into a bag of pattern blocks containing only blue rhombi and red trapezoids and pull some out. Your partner tells you that you have taken 10 pieces, and if each piece was exchanged for the correct number of triangles, you would have 27 triangles. How many rhombi and how many trapezoids did you take?

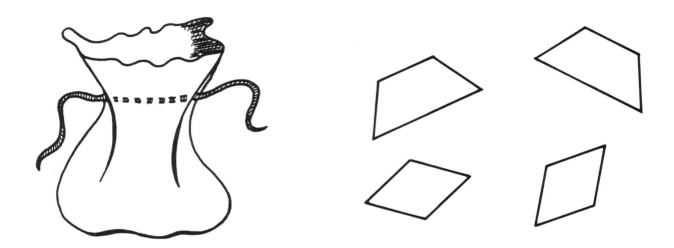

How many of each kind would you have taken if all the pieces could be exchanged for 25 triangles?

EXPLORE MORE: Suppose you put your hand in the bag and this time you grab 20 pieces that could be exchanged for 51 triangles. How many blue rhombi and how many red trapezoids did you take? Use the table to help you.

Number of blue rhombi	Number of trapezoids	Number of △ replacing the blue rhombi	Number of △ replacing the trapezoids	Total number of triangles
20	0	40	0	40
19	1	38	3	41
18	2	36	6	42

MORE GRAB BAG FUN

Suppose, without looking, you put your hand into a bag of pattern blocks containing only trapezoids and hexagons and pull some out. Your partner tells you that you have taken 17 pieces, and if each piece was exchanged for the correct number of triangles, you would have 75 triangles. How many trapezoids and how many hexagons did you take?

How many triangles would you need to exchange for 10 trapezoids and 7 hexagons?

EXPLORE MORE: Suppose you put your hand into the bag and this time you grab fewer than 20 pieces. Your partner tells you that you have picked the same number of hexagons and trapezoids and that they can be exchanged for 45 triangles. How many of each block did you pick? Use the table to help you.

Number of hexagons	Number of trapezoids	Number of △ replacing the hexagons	Number of △ replacing the trapezoids	Total number of triangles
1	1	6	3	9
2	2	12	6	18

BUILDING PATTERNS I

Construct each of the following patterns with pattern blocks. Then decide what comes next. Record your solutions. Since there is often more than one possibility, be ready to explain your choice.

1.

2.

3.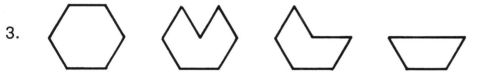

4.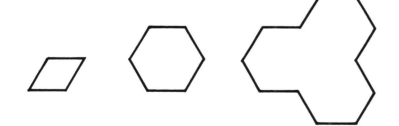

5.

EXPLORE MORE: Create a pattern of your own. Build and record the first four parts of your pattern. Ask someone to predict what comes next.

BUILDING PATTERNS II

Construct each of the following patterns with pattern blocks. Then decide what comes next. Record your solutions. Since there is often more than one possibility, be ready to explain your choice.

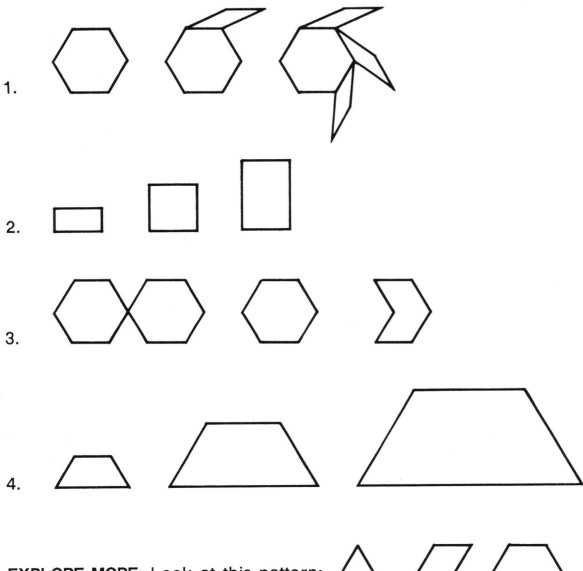

1.

2.

3.

4.

EXPLORE MORE: Look at this pattern:

Dana says each one of the choices below could complete the pattern. Explain why each is possible. Can you think of another choice?

A

B

C

D

Exploring with Pattern Blocks © 1989 Cuisenaire Company of America, Inc.

TRIANGULAR NUMBERS

Make triangles of different sizes as shown below. (The shaded triangles are empty spaces.)

A

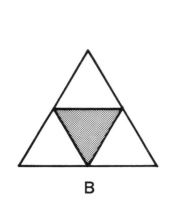

B

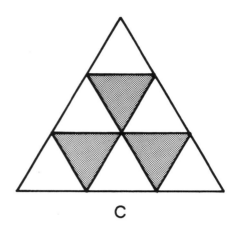

C

Count the number of green triangles needed for each one. How many green triangles are needed to build triangle D (the next biggest similar triangle)? Record.

A = _____   B = _____   C = _____   D = _____

What patterns do you see?

For each successive triangle formed, a new base can be added, increasing the length by one. Using this pattern, how many green triangles would you need for triangles E and F (the next biggest similar triangles)? Complete the table.

The numbers in the sequence 1, 3, 6, 10, ... are called triangular numbers. Why?

Triangle	Number of green triangles	Total number of green triangles
A	1	1
B	1 + 2	3
C	1 + 2 + 3	6
D		
E		
F		

EXPLORE MORE: Make the same triangular patterns but this time do not leave any spaces between the green triangles. For example, your first triangle will use 1 green triangle, the second triangle will use 4, and the third will use 9. Make a table like the one above. Fill in your table for at least 6 triangles. What's the number sequence now?

SQUARE NUMBERS

Make squares of different sizes as shown below.

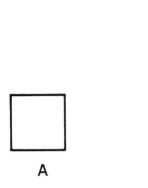

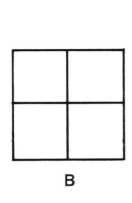

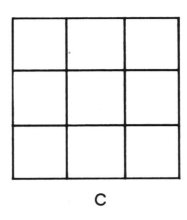

A   B   C

Count the number of orange squares needed for each one. How many orange squares are needed to build square D (the next biggest square)? Record.

A = _____   B = _____   C = _____   D = _____

What patterns do you see?

For each successive square formed, the length of the side increases by one. Using this pattern, how many orange squares are needed for squares E and F (the next biggest squares)?

Complete the table.

The numbers in the sequence 1, 4, 9, 16 ... are called square numbers. Why?

Square	Number of orange squares	Total number of orange squares
A	1	1
B	1 + 3	4
C	1 + 3 + 5	9
D		
E		
F		

EXPLORE MORE: How many odd numbers are added to get the fourth square number? the fifth? the ninth? the tenth? What is the sum of the first 50 odd numbers? Which square number is this?

Exploring with Pattern Blocks © 1989 Cuisenaire Company of America, Inc.

TRIANGULAR OR SQUARE NUMBERS

Build the next biggest shape similar to each of the pattern blocks shown below.
How many of each block do you need? Record.
How many blocks would you use each time if you continued to build bigger and bigger similar shapes? Record.

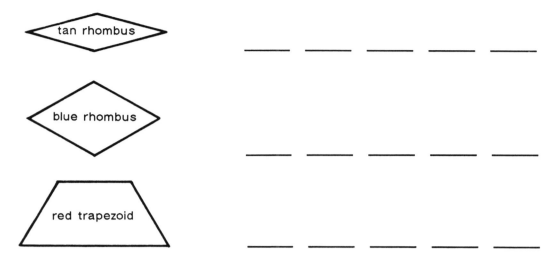

___ ___ ___ ___ ___ ___

___ ___ ___ ___ ___

___ ___ ___ ___ ___

Do the number of pattern blocks used produce the sequence of triangular or square numbers? Why?

Investigate building bigger and bigger similar shapes with the yellow hexagon. Describe what you find.

EXPLORE MORE: Building rectangles produces a sequence of rectangular numbers. Use orange squares to build rectangles A and B. Then build the next two rectangles in the pattern.

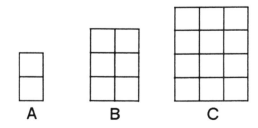

Complete the table. Predict the seventh rectangular number in this sequence. Look for a pattern that will help you predict any number in the sequence.

Rectangle	Dimensions	Total number of orange squares
A	1 x 2	2
B	2 x 3	6
C		
D		
E		
F		

PATTERN BLOCK SYMMETRY

A line of symmetry is a line that divides a figure so that each side is identical to the other except for position. The triangle below is re-drawn several times to show its three lines of symmetry. For each of the pattern block shapes, sketch all the lines of symmetry. Check with a mirror.

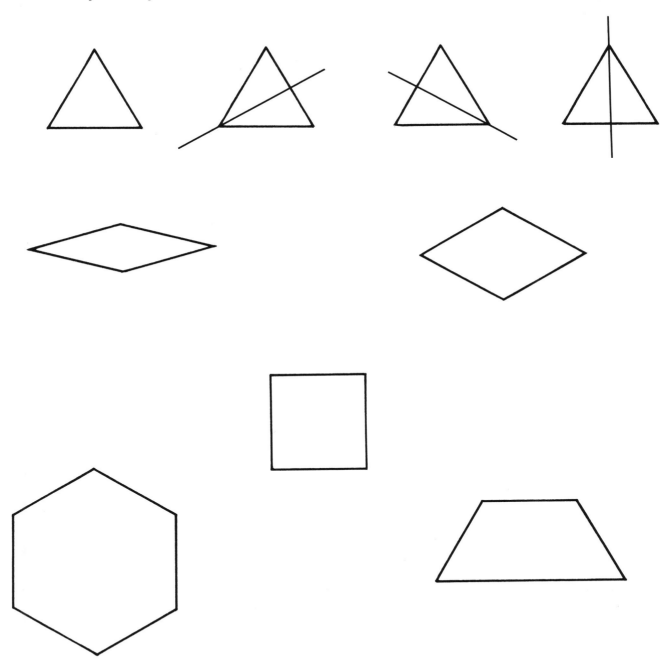

EXPLORE MORE: Put two or more pattern blocks together to form a figure with one line of symmetry. Sketch your figure and its line of symmetry. Put two or more pattern blocks together to form a figure with two or more lines of symmetry. Sketch your figure and its lines of symmetry.

Exploring with Pattern Blocks © 1989 Cuisenaire Company of America, Inc.

FOLDED SHAPES

These pattern block designs were folded along the indicated line of symmetry. Imagine what each design would look like unfolded and sketch it. Check your thinking by placing a mirror on the line of symmetry.

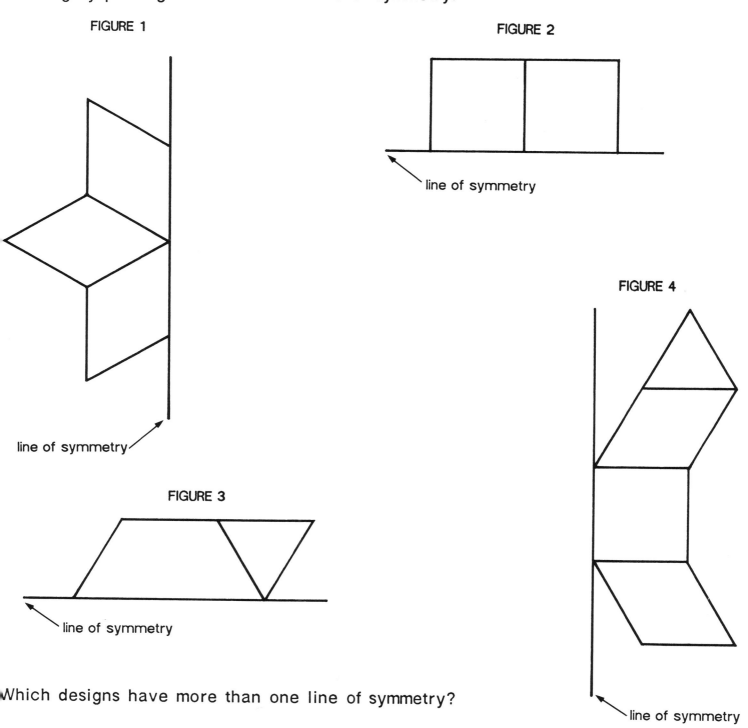

FIGURE 1

line of symmetry

FIGURE 2

line of symmetry

FIGURE 3

line of symmetry

FIGURE 4

line of symmetry

Which designs have more than one line of symmetry?

EXPLORE MORE: Make an original design having only one line of symmetry. Then fold it along its line of symmetry and record the result. Make a design that has two lines of symmetry. Fold it along either line of symmetry. Record the result. Ask someone to build your original designs from your recordings.

SIMPLE SYMMETRY

Use pattern blocks to cover each figure below. Sketch the blocks you used. Sketch all the lines of symmetry.

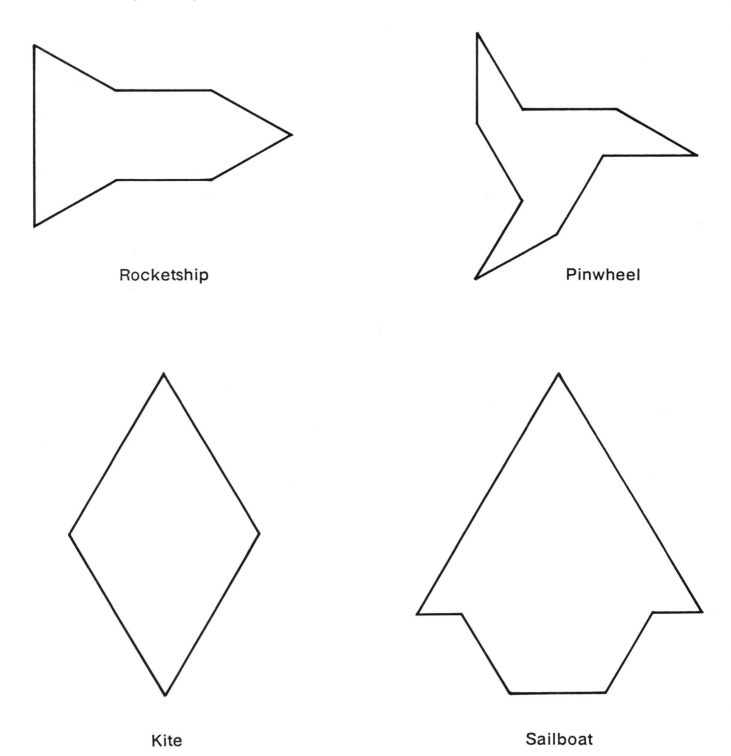

Rocketship

Pinwheel

Kite

Sailboat

EXPLORE MORE: Cover the figures above in a different way, if possible. Do the lines of symmetry change?

Exploring with Pattern Blocks © 1989 Cuisenaire Company of America, Inc.

COPY CAT

Look at designs A, B and C. Build each one as if you were seeing it in a mirror. Use a mirror to check what you've built. Record what you've built. The first one has been started for you.

A

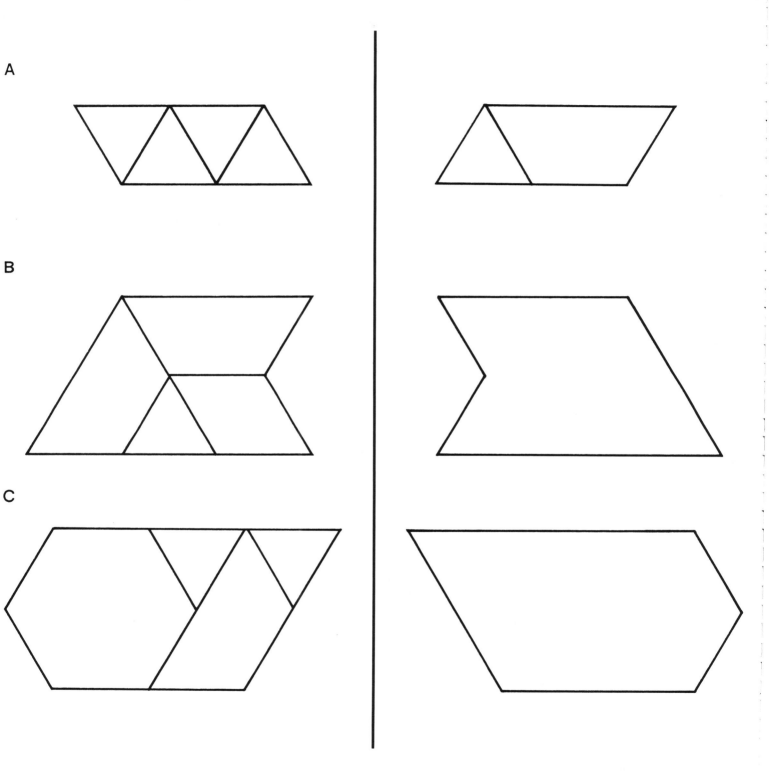

B

C

EXPLORE MORE: Make a design and sketch it. Ask someone to copy it as if he or she were seeing it in a mirror.

Exploring with Pattern Blocks © 1989 Cuisenaire Company of America, Inc.

SCRAMBLED IMAGES

Place pattern blocks on each pair of designs below. Each pair was a mirror image until some of the blocks were scrambled. Move the blocks within the given outlines to make a completely new design and its mirror image.

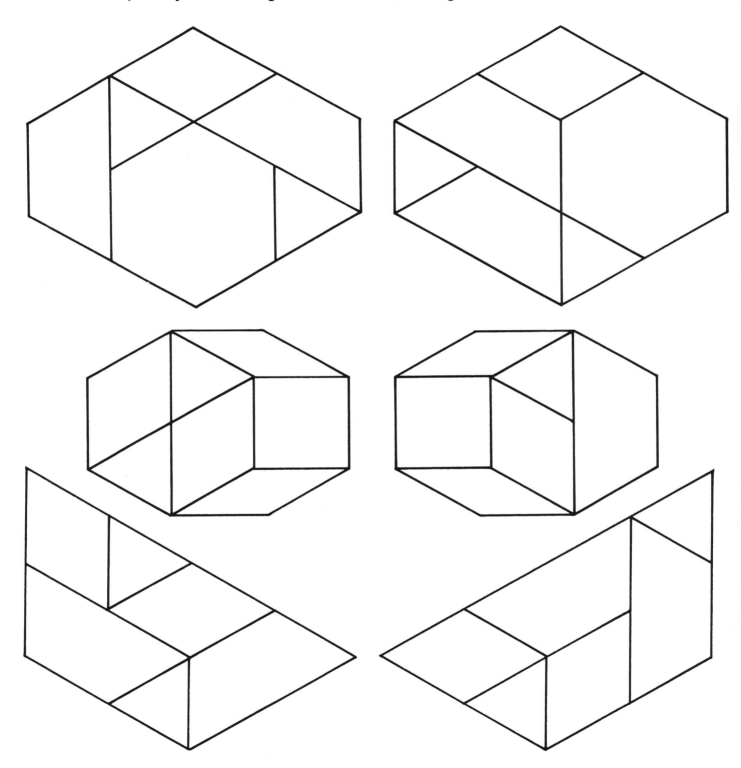

EXPLORE MORE: Choose one of the above outlines. Using the indicated pieces, make another design that fits the outline. How many ways can you scramble the pieces within the same outline? Sketch all your designs. Compare with a partner.

Exploring with Pattern Blocks © 1989 Cuisenaire Company of America, Inc.

THE FLIP SIDE

Use pattern blocks to copy each figure. What would each figure look like if it were flipped once along the indicated line? Sketch it in the outline provided. What would it look like if it were flipped twice? five times? eight times? Is there a pattern? Does it always work?

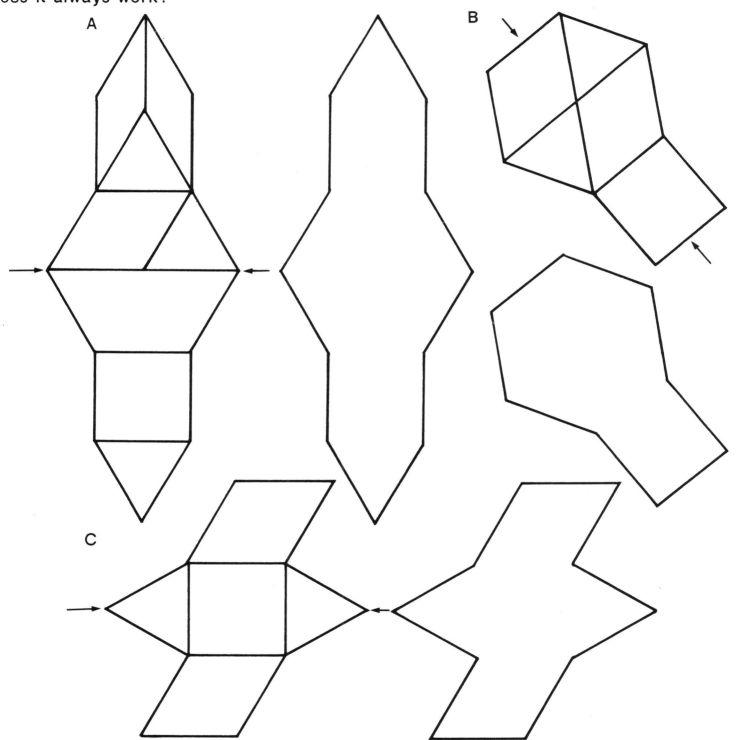

EXPLORE MORE: Construct a figure that does not change when it is flipped.

THE FLIP SIDE ONE MORE TIME

Use pattern blocks to build each figure. What would each figure look like if it was flipped once along the indicated line? Record and color the flip side on the grid below.

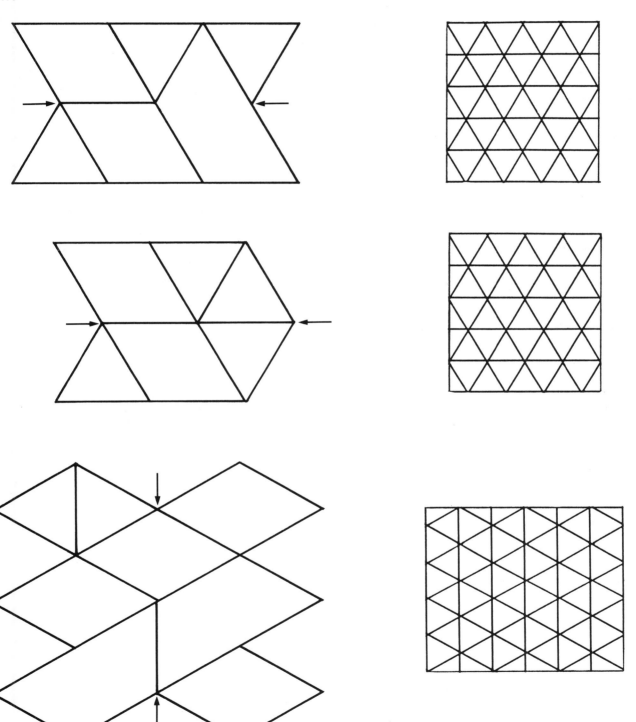

EXPLORE MORE: Flip each figure about any line you choose. Compare it to the original figure. What do you find?

ONE GOOD TURN DESERVES ANOTHER

Rotate each design clockwise the indicated amount. Copy the resulting figure on the small grid.

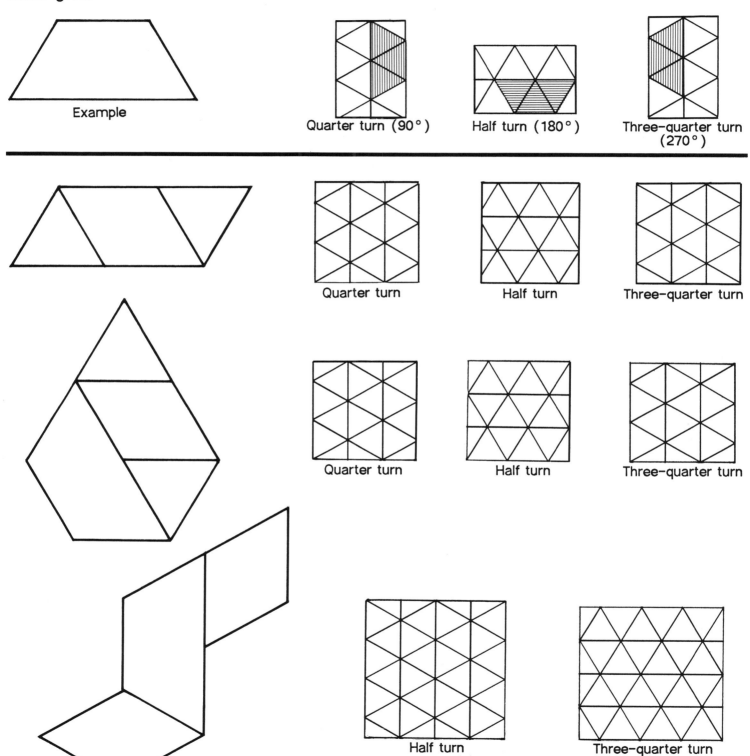

Example

Quarter turn (90°)   Half turn (180°)   Three-quarter turn (270°)

Quarter turn   Half turn   Three-quarter turn

Quarter turn   Half turn   Three-quarter turn

Half turn   Three-quarter turn

EXPLORE MORE: Make a design that looks the same no matter which turn (quarter, half, or three-quarter) you make.

Exploring with Pattern Blocks © 1989 Cuisenaire Company of America, Inc.

ANOTHER TURN

Visualize how the figure would appear when rotated as indicated. Shade the resulting figure on the grid. Check your prediction by using pattern blocks.

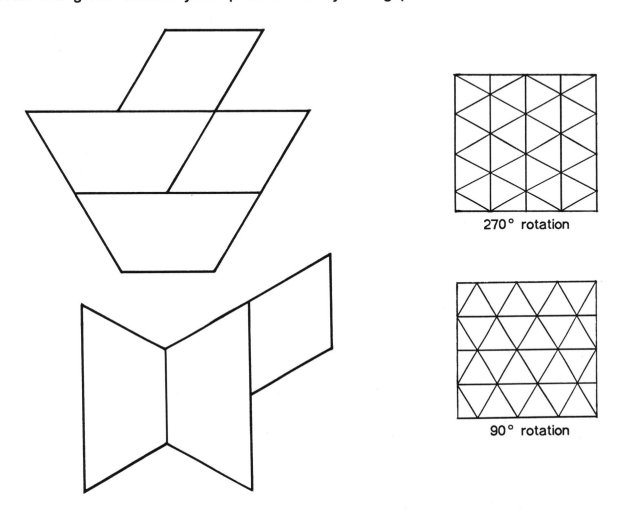

270° rotation

90° rotation

For each figure, indicate the amount it has been rotated.

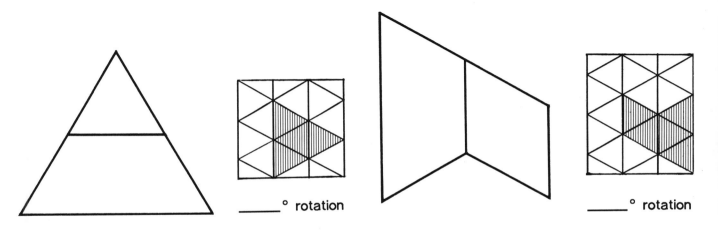

_____° rotation

_____° rotation

EXPLORE MORE: Create a figure that looks the same as the original when it is rotated 180° and 360°, but not the same after 90° or 270°. Record both your figure and its rotations.

CREATIVE SYMMETRY I

Using the pattern blocks shown, make designs that have the indicated lines of symmetry. Sketch each design in the space provided.

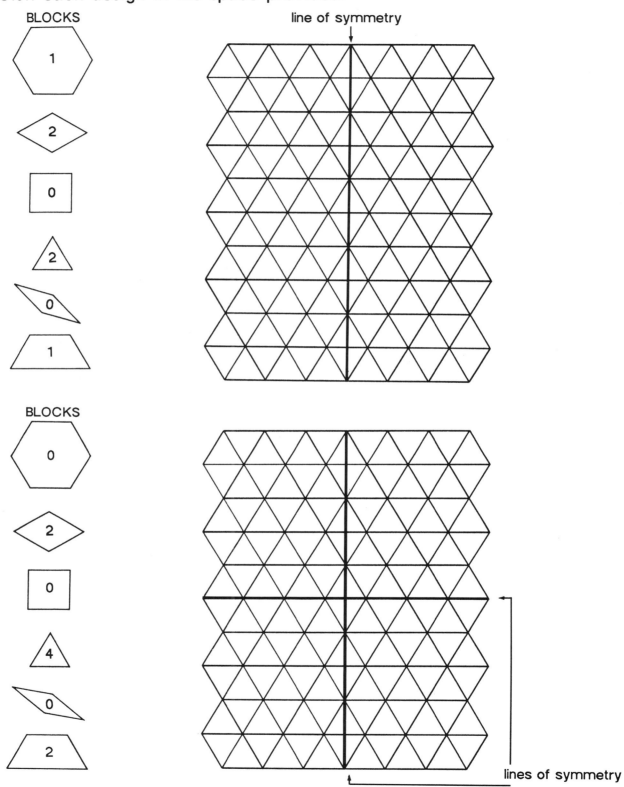

EXPLORE MORE: Using two of each pattern block shape, can you make a figure with 0 lines of symmetry; with 1 line of symmetry; with 2; with 3? Sketch what you make.

CREATIVE SYMMETRY II

Using the pattern blocks shown, make designs that have the indicated lines of symmetry. Sketch each in the space provided and draw the lines of symmetry.

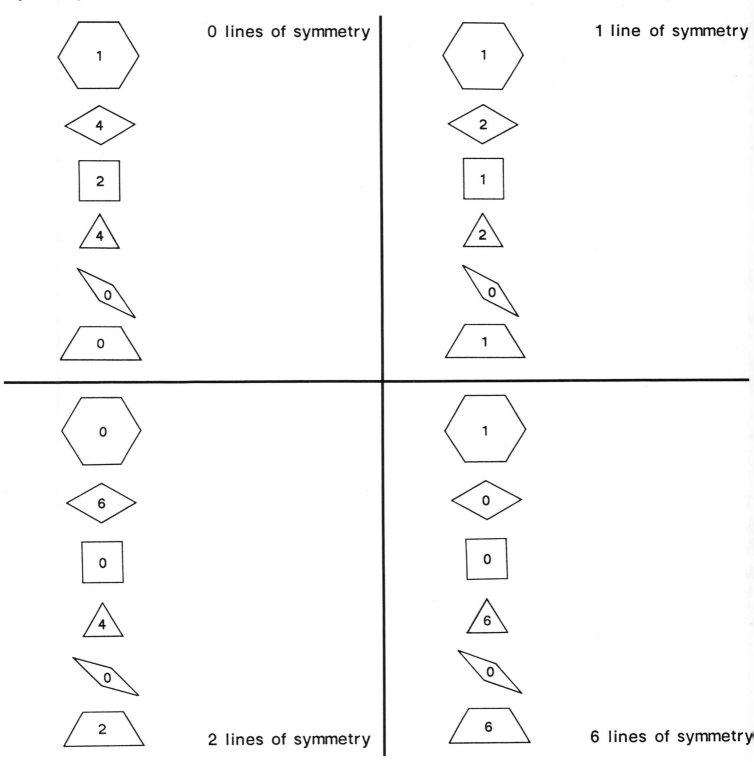

0 lines of symmetry

1 line of symmetry

2 lines of symmetry

6 lines of symmetry

EXPLORE MORE: Grab a handful of pattern blocks. Make a design with as many lines of symmetry as possible. Sketch the design. Draw in the lines of symmetry.

Exploring with Pattern Blocks © 1989 Cuisenaire Company of America, Inc.

PACKAGES

If the green triangle has an area of one, what is the area of the package shown?

Cover the package with green triangles. Now rearrange the triangles into a different shape. Draw it on the grid.

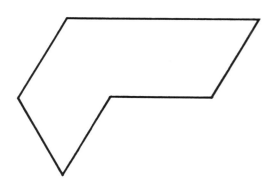

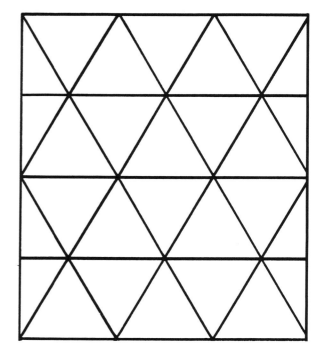

What is the area of your new package?

If the length of a side of the green triangle is one unit, what is the perimeter of the original package?

What is the perimeter of your new package?

Double the number of green triangles you just used. Make a package with them.

What is its area?

What is its perimeter?

When you doubled the number of triangles, what happened to the total area? What happened to the total perimeter?

EXPLORE MORE: Use triangles to make a package whose perimeter is double that of the original package. What is its perimeter? What is its area? How does it compare to the area of the original package?

MORE PACKAGES

If the blue rhombus has an area of 2, make a package with an area of 10. If the length of one side of the rhombus is 1 unit, what is the perimeter of your package?

Draw your package on the grid. Label it A.

Make a new package with an area of 10 but a different perimeter. What is its perimeter? Draw your package on the grid. Label it B.

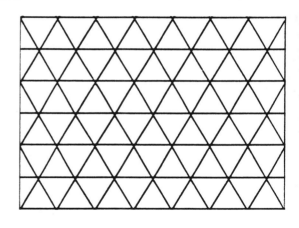

If the blue rhombus has an area of 2 and its side has a length of 1 unit, draw packages to match the given information.

Area = 8   Perimeter = 10

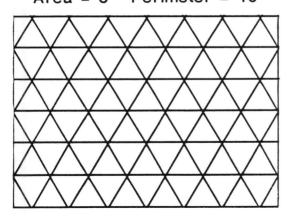

Area = 6   Perimeter = 8

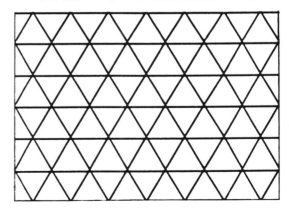

Area = 12   Perimeter = 10

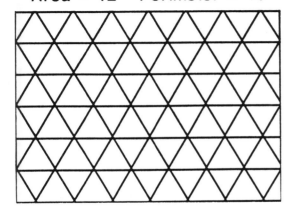

Can two figures with the same perimeter have different areas?

Can two figures with the same area have different perimeters?

EXPLORE MORE: Make a package that has an area of 8 and a perimeter that is not 10 units. What is its perimeter?

REWRAP

The length of one side of the triangle is equal to one unit. Take four triangles and make different shaped packages. The triangles must touch completely along at least one side. Sketch the package with the largest perimeter. Sketch the package with the smallest perimeter. Do the same for the other blocks.

SKETCH

Shape	Take	Smallest perimeter	Largest perimeter
△ green triangle	4	____ units	____ units
◇ blue rhombus	4	____ units	____ units
⬭ red trapezoid	4	____ units	____ units

If the green triangle has an area of 1, what is the area of each package you sketched? Did the package with the smallest perimeter have the smallest area?

EXPLORE MORE: Do the activity above using 5 of each shape.

Exploring with Pattern Blocks © 1989 Cuisenaire Company of America, Inc.

BLOCKS AND CORNERS

Place the corresponding pattern blocks on the outlines below. Trace the edge of each pattern block with your finger, stopping at the corners. Two edges having a corner in common form an angle. Record below the number of angles in each pattern block.

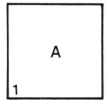

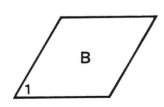

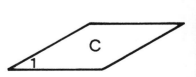

Number of angles _____

Number of angles _____

Number of angles _____

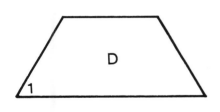

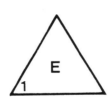

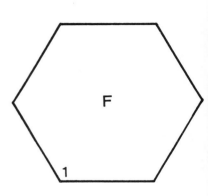

Number of angles _____

Number of angles _____

Number of angles _____

Which pattern blocks have all its angles congruent?

One way to find out is to rotate each pattern block, trying to fit every angle of each block into corner number 1. Only the angles that fit exactly into the corner are congruent.

EXPLORE MORE: Look at the congruent angles in the hexagon. Does any other shape have an angle of the same measure? Use your pattern blocks to find out which shapes have angles congruent to those in the hexagon.

Exploring with Pattern Blocks © 1989 Cuisenaire Company of America, Inc.

BLOCKS, CORNERS AND INTERSECTIONS

Place the corner of the orange pattern block at the intersection of the two dotted lines. These lines intersect forming right angles. How many right angles does the square contain? Do any of the other pattern blocks have right angles?

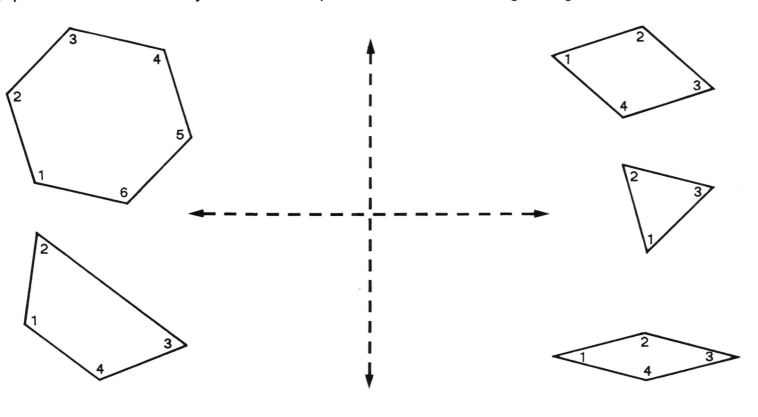

Next to each numbered angle, write G if you think the angle measure is greater than a right angle and L if you think it is less.

You can check your findings by placing the corners of each pattern block at the intersection of the dotted lines.

EXPLORE MORE: Examine each angle in the shapes below. Decide if each angle is greater than, less than, or the same as a right angle.

A   B   C

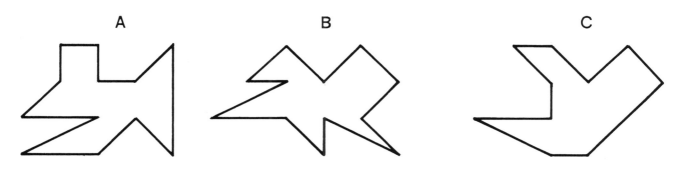

Exploring with Pattern Blocks © 1989 Cuisenaire Company of America, Inc.

VIEW FROM A RIGHT ANGLE

Angles *greater than* right angles are called OBTUSE angles. Which pattern blocks have obtuse angles?

Angles *less than* right angles are called ACUTE angles. Which pattern blocks have acute angles?

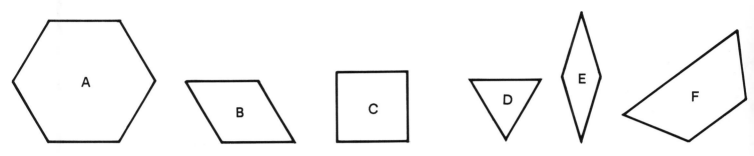

Which pattern blocks have *only* obtuse angles?
Which pattern blocks have *only* acute angles?
Which pattern blocks have *both* kinds of angles?
Which obtuse angle has the greatest measure?
Which acute angle has the smallest measure?

Two right angles sharing a common corner form a STRAIGHT angle.

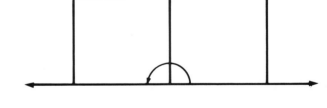

Straight angles can also be formed by placing the corners of two or more blocks together. One example is shown. Find at least 5 more ways to make a straight angle using two or more pattern blocks.

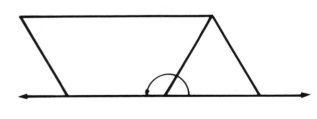

EXPLORE MORE: Place the corners of two or more blocks together to form a RIGHT angle. How many different ways can you make a right angle? Record your findings.

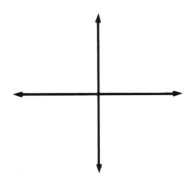

FORMING FLOWERS

Flowers of one color can be formed by making straight angles above and below a straight line.

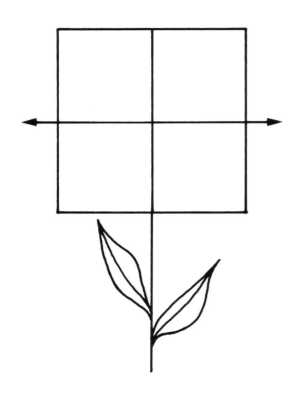

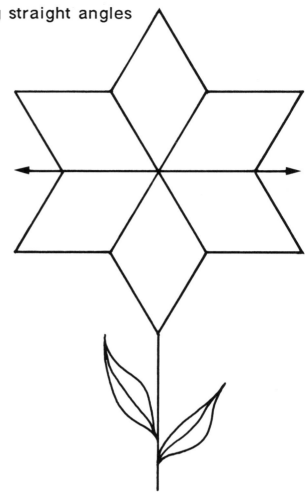

Place one acute angle of the tan rhombus on the line at the right. How many tan rhombi do you think you need to make a one-color flower? Complete the top half of the tan flower, then make its reflection. How many tan rhombi did it take?

As each angle in the center of the one-color flowers gets smaller, do you need more blocks or fewer blocks to make the flower?

Make an original two-color flower. Record.

Make an original three-color flower. Record.

EXPLORE MORE: Using the method described above, try to make a flower with petals of 4 colors; of 5 colors. Is it possible? Why? Compare all the flowers. What do they have in common?

DEGREE POWER

A circle is the geometric figure that all one-color flowers (p. 44) have in common. Put 4 orange squares on the circle below. The central angle of the circle contains 360°.

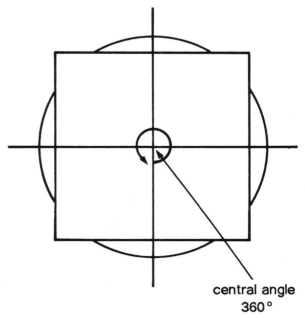

Since the central angle of the circle contains 4 right angles, how many degrees are in each right angle?

Since 3 acute angles of the tan rhombus make a right angle, how many degrees are in each acute angle?

central angle
360°

Using the acute angle of the tan rhombus, find the measure of each of the following angles.

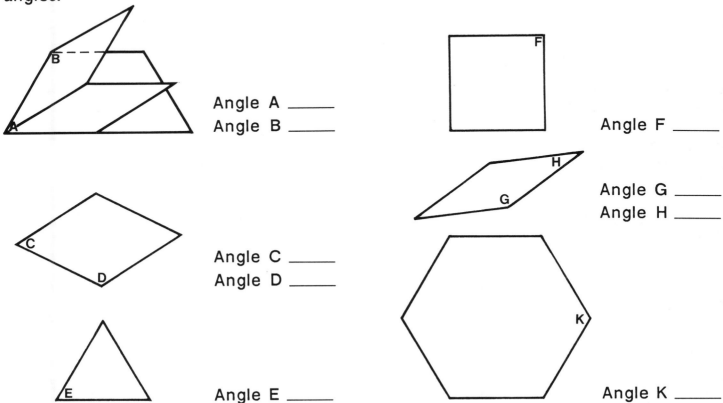

Angle A _____
Angle B _____

Angle C _____
Angle D _____

Angle E _____

Angle F _____

Angle G _____
Angle H _____

Angle K _____

EXPLORE MORE: What is the measure of a straight angle? Prove your answer using the pattern blocks.

Exploring with Pattern Blocks © 1989 Cuisenaire Company of America, Inc.

FORMULATING FORMULAS

Cover the figure shown with orange squares.

If the orange square has an area of 1, what is the area of the figure?
How many squares wide is it?
How many squares long is it?

Take the blocks you used to cover this figure and rearrange them into another rectangular figure.

What is its area?
What is its width?
What is its length?

Rearrange the blocks again. Can you form a third rectangular figure whose dimensions are different from the first two?

Record all your information in the chart below.

Using 8 blocks, build all the rectangles possible.
What size rectangles can you form? Record below.

Total Area	Rectangle 1		Rectangle 2		Rectangle 3		Rectangle 4	
	Width	Length	Width	Length	Width	Length	Width	Length
6								
8								

Make a rectangle with a length of 4 and a width of 3. What is its area? How many squares did you use? Rearrange the same number of squares to form a different rectangle. What is its area? its length? its width? Continue rearranging the blocks until you have made all the rectangles possible. Record the area, length, and width of each arrangement.

Write a formula that will give the area when you know the length and width of a rectangle.

If you are given a particular area, such as 20, how would you know which rectangles are possible?

EXPLORE MORE: Predict the dimensions of all possible rectangles with an area of 24 square units. Check by using the orange blocks.

Exploring with Pattern Blocks © 1989 Cuisenaire Company of America, Inc.

THE TRIANGLE CONNECTION

Below are all the possible arrangements of triangles taken 2 at a time, 3 at a time, and 4 at a time. In every arrangement, the triangles touch completely along at least one side.

2 triangles    3 triangles

4 triangles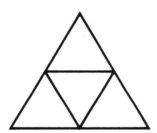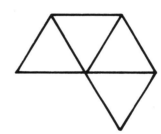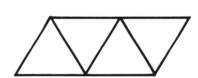

Using pattern blocks, make all the different arrangements possible with 5 triangles. Be sure the triangles touch completely on at least one side. Record on triangular grid paper. If a shape can be flipped and/or turned to fit exactly on another shape, it is not considered to be different.

EXPLORE MORE: How many arrangements can you make with 2 blue rhombi, using the rule that the rhombi must touch completely along at least one side. With 3 blue rhombi? Record on triangular grid paper. How do the number of arrangements using green triangles compare to the number of arrangements using blue rhombi?

Exploring with Pattern Blocks © 1989 Cuisenaire Company of America, Inc.

PUZZLING PENTOMINOES

Below are all the possible arrangements of orange squares taken 2 at a time, 3 at a time, and 4 at a time. In every arrangement, the squares touch completely along at least one side.

Dominoes (2 squares)

Trominoes (3 squares)

Tetrominoes (4 squares)

Using pattern blocks, make all the different arrangements possible with 5 squares (pentominoes). Be sure the squares touch completely on at least one side. Record on square grid paper. If a pentomino can be flipped and/or turned to fit on another pentomino, it is not considered to be different.

How many different pentominoes did you find?

All the pentominoes have the same area (5 square units). Do they all have the same perimeter?

EXPLORE MORE: Which pentominoes do you think will fold up into an open box? Put a B on the square which you think will be the bottom of each box. Then, cut out the pentominoes and fold them to check.

Exploring with Pattern Blocks © 1989 Cuisenaire Company of America, Inc.

THE RHOMBUS CONNECTION

Below are all the possible arrangements of blue rhombi taken 2 at a time and 3 at a time. In every arrangement, the rhombi touch completely along at least one side.

2 rhombi

3 rhombi

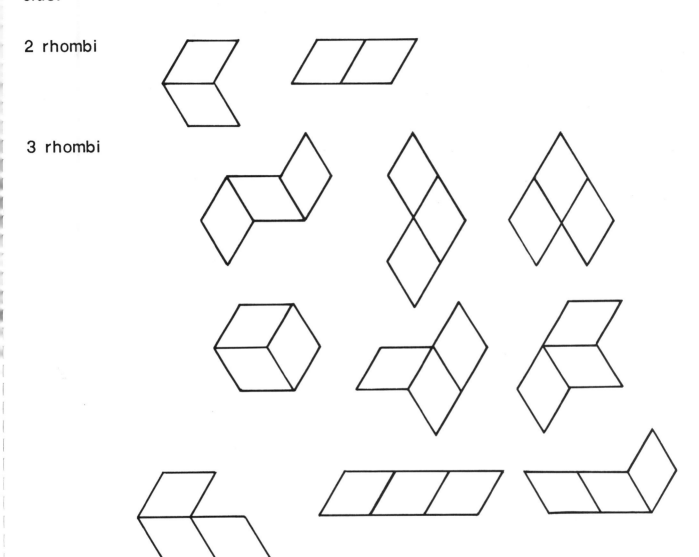

Using pattern blocks, make all the different arrangements possible with 4 blue rhombi. Be sure the blocks touch completely on at least one side. Record on triangular grid paper. If a shape can be flipped and/or turned to fit exactly on another one, it is not considered to be different.

How many different arrangements did you find?

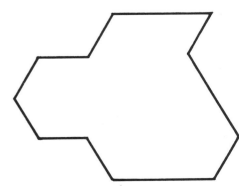

EXPLORE MORE: Label each arrangement with a letter. All arrangements have the same area. Which have the same perimeter? What is the smallest perimeter? What is the largest perimeter? Which 3 arrangements fit together to make a shape similar to the figure shown at the right? What is its area and perimeter?

Exploring with Pattern Blocks © 1989 Cuisenaire Company of America, Inc.

FORCE OUT
(An Activity for 2 or 3)

Materials: Pattern blocks of 2 or 3 different colors; the gameboard below.

Object: To be the last person to place a pattern block on the gameboard

Directions: Players each select pattern blocks of one color. Players take turns placing a block in any square on the gameboard, according to the following rules:
    1. The same color cannot appear in the same row or column or along the principal diagonals.
    2. Play continues until a player cannot place a block.

EXPLORE MORE: Is it possible to cover the entire 3 x 3 gameboard according to the rules given above? Will there always be a force out? It is possible to cover a 4 x 4 gameboard using four colors and the rules given above. Draw a gameboard showing one way this can be done. Play a 4-person game using a 4 x 4 gameboard and pattern blocks in 4 different colors.

Exploring with Pattern Blocks © 1989 Cuisenaire Company of America, Inc.

WRAPPING FIGURES

Start with the pattern block pieces shown below. Using the same kind of piece, wrap the original block by adding a layer of pieces around it, filling in corners where necessary, to make a larger similiar shape. How many pieces does it take? Repeat the procedure two more times. Record your answers and sketch your results. Predict what the results will be for a third wrap. Check your prediction. Triangles have been started for you.

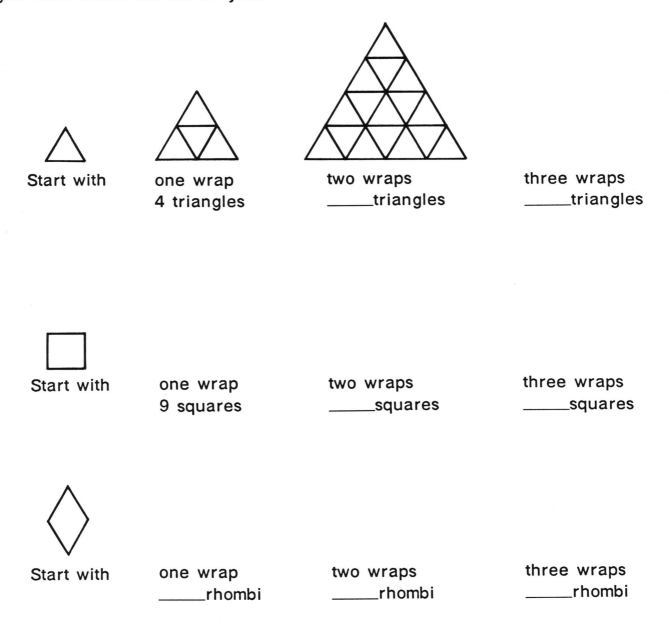

Start with   one wrap   two wraps   three wraps
                  4 triangles   _____triangles   _____triangles

Start with   one wrap   two wraps   three wraps
                  9 squares   _____squares   _____squares

Start with   one wrap   two wraps   three wraps
                  _____rhombi   _____rhombi   _____rhombi

EXPLORE MORE: Try to wrap each of the remaining pattern block pieces to form similar figures. Which ones work? Which ones do not work?

Exploring with Pattern Blocks © 1989 Cuisenaire Company of America, Inc.

SUM ANGLES

The right angle (90°) of the square can be formed with 3 acute angles of tan rhombi. Therefore, the measure of each acute angle of a tan rhombus is 30°.

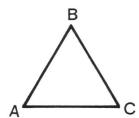

Find the measure of each angle of triangle ABC.

Angle A= _____

Angle B= _____

Angle C= _____

The sum of the measures of the angles of the triangle is _____.

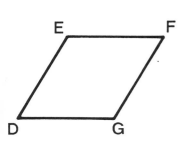

James says, "The blue rhombus is equivalent to 2 triangles. Therefore, the measure of its angles is 360°."

Find the measure of each angle of rhombus DEFG.

Angle D= _____

Angle E= _____

Angle F= _____

Angle G= _____

The sum of the measures of the angles of the rhombus is _____.

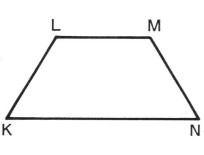

Brian says, "The trapezoid is equivalent to the rhombus and the triangle. Therefore the measure of its angles is 360° plus 180° or 540°."

Find the measure of each angle of trapezoid KLMN.

Angle K= _____

Angle L= _____

Angle M= _____

Angle N= _____

Is the sum 540°? Explain.

Find the sum of the measure of the angles of the tan rhombus; of the square.

Are the sums of the measures of the angles of all pattern block quadrilaterals the same?

EXPLORE MORE: The yellow hexagon equals 2 trapezoids or 6 triangles. Predict the sum of the measure of its angles. Using the tan rhombus, find the measure of each angle. Find the sum of its angles.

Exploring with Pattern Blocks © 1989 Cuisenaire Company of America, Inc.

HIDDEN WONDERS

Look carefully at each of the following grids. The indicated pieces fit exactly into each grid with no overlapping. Locate the pieces on the grid and color them, each in a different color.

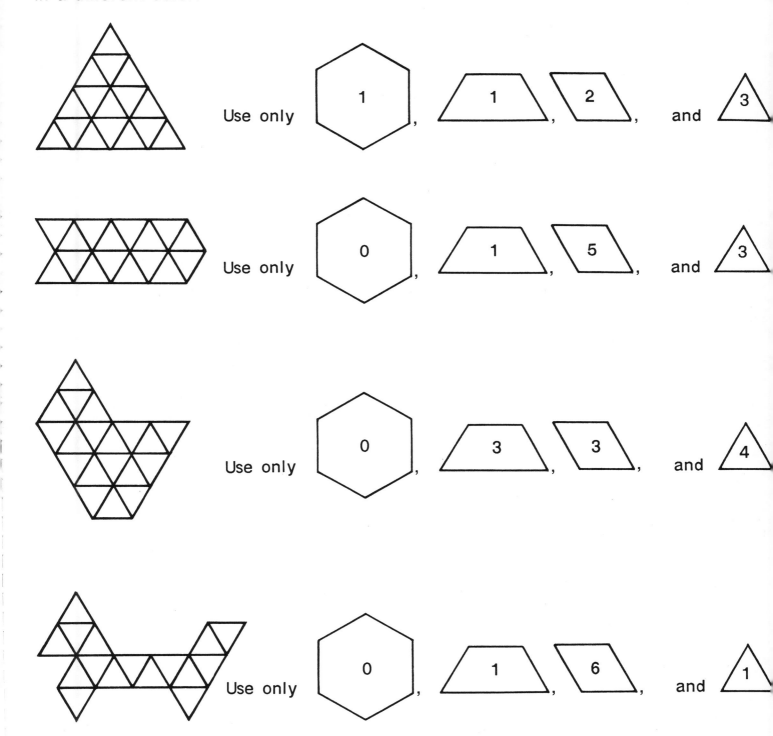

EXPLORE MORE: Draw your own hidden wonders. Try to draw a shape that can be covered entirely with hexagons; with trapezoids but not hexagons.

Exploring with Pattern Blocks © 1989 Cuisenaire Company of America, Inc.

HIDDEN WONDERS TOO

Each puzzle piece below will fit exactly into at least one of the grids shown. Match each piece to a grid and draw it on the grid. There is one piece per grid and every piece is used.

PUZZLE PIECES   GRIDS

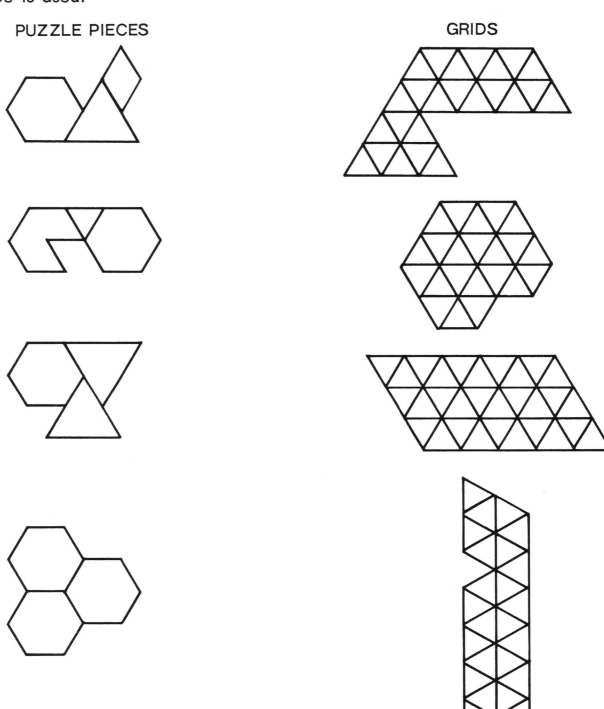

EXPLORE MORE: Take the four puzzle pieces above and make one shape, using each of them once. Sketch the outline of the shape on triangular grid paper. Ask someone to locate each puzzle piece on your grid and color each with a different color.

PUZZLER

Each shape has been cut into four pieces and scrambled with a fifth unrelated piece. Put an X on each of the four pieces that could fit together to form the original shape.

SHAPES   PUZZLE PIECES

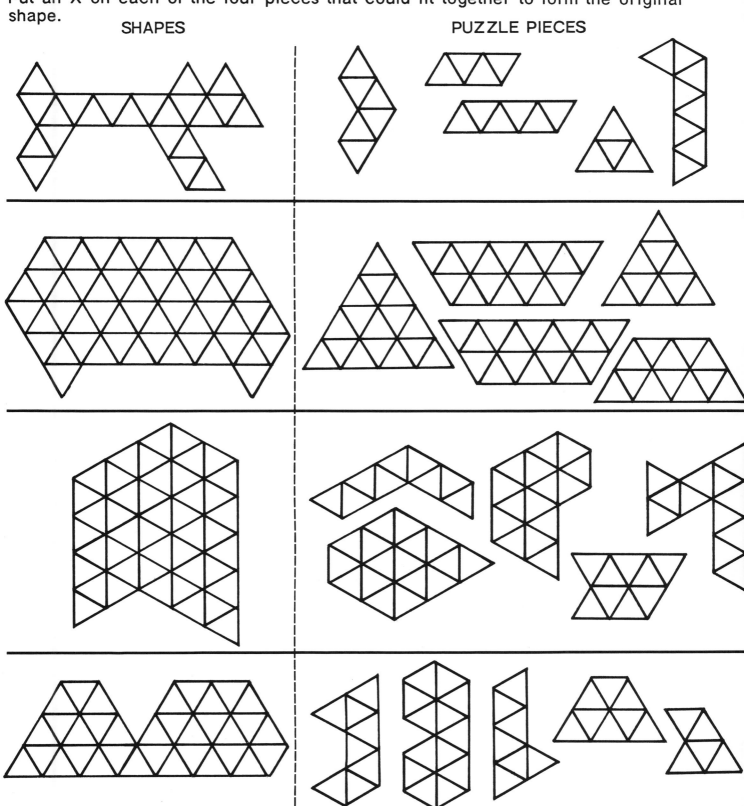

EXPLORE: Make your own puzzler and give it to a friend.

Exploring with Pattern Blocks © 1989 Cuisenaire Company of America, Inc.

DOUBLE VISION

Reflect each figure twice—first about the line numbered 1 and then about the line numbered 2. Record the results of each reflection on the small grids. Each triangle on the grid represents a green pattern block triangle.

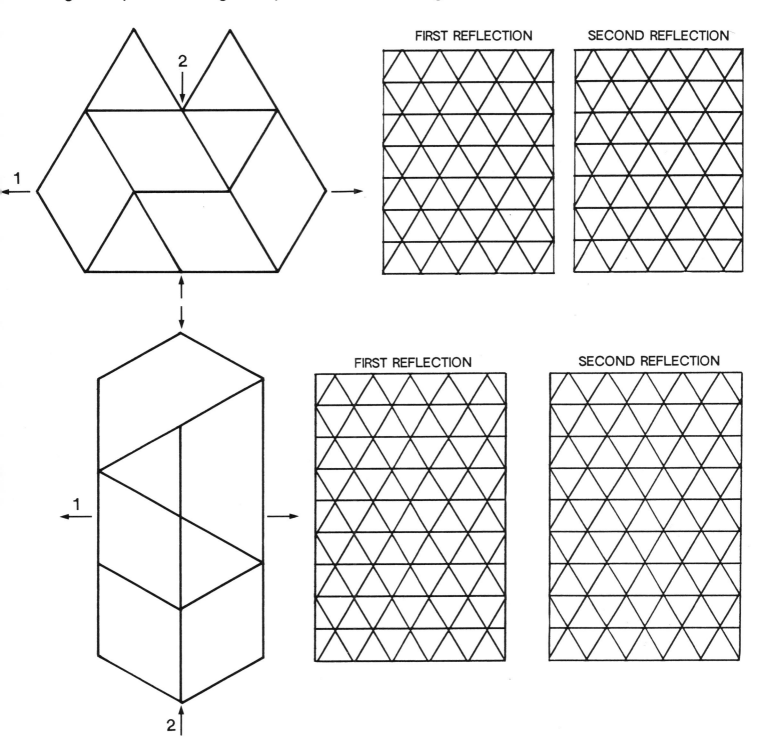

FIRST REFLECTION   SECOND REFLECTION

FIRST REFLECTION   SECOND REFLECTION

EXPLORE MORE: Use a small grid. Make a design by coloring pattern block pieces on your grid. Show two lines of reflection. Ask a friend to copy your design with pattern blocks and make the reflections about the 2 lines. Check with a mirror.

Exploring with Pattern Blocks © 1989 Cuisenaire Company of America, Inc.

CLUES

Blocks were placed in a box. Frances put her hand inside the box, picked a block, and described it. She did this 3 times. Guess which block she had each time.

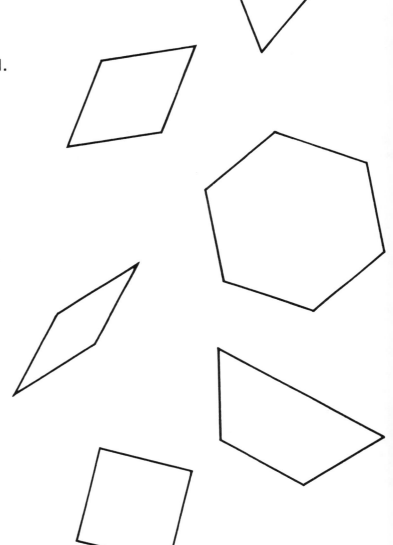

BLOCK A

It has four sides.
It has obtuse and acute angles.
Only one pair of opposite sides is parallel.
Which block is it?

BLOCK B

It has fewer than 6 sides.
All of its sides and angles are congruent.
It has no right angles.
Which block is it?

BLOCK C

It has more than one line of symmetry.
It has more than 3 sides.
It has obtuse angles.
It's not a parallelogram.
Which block is it?

FIND MY BLOCK

Dana, Sandi, Vincent and Bill each selected a different pattern block. Dana's block had all congruent sides and angles. Bill's block had obtuse and acute angles. One of the blocks had only 3 sides. Vincent's block had just one line of symmetry. Sandi's block had an area equivalent to two triangles. Who had which block?

EXPLORE MORE: Write your own pattern block riddles. Write one that can be answered with 3 clues. Write one that needs 4 clues. Ask someone to solve your riddles.

Pg. 5   Startime

Objectives:
To recognize each kind of pattern block.
To use the geometric names of the pattern blocks.
To learn the relationships among the pattern blocks.

Answers:
Answers may vary.

Explore More:
The star can be made with 6 rhombi and 0 triangles.

Pg. 6   Gretles

Objectives:
To recognize each kind of pattern block.
To use the geometric names of the pattern blocks.
To learn the relationships among the pattern blocks.

Answers:
No; no; no; yes

Pg. 7   Cover Three

Objectives:
To discover all the ways to make a hexagon.
To learn the relationships among the pattern blocks.

Pg. 8   Countdown 10, 9, 8, ..., 1!

Objectives:
To make similar designs.
To develop visualization skills.
To replicate patterns from memory.

Pg. 9   Space Station

Objectives:
To learn the relationships among the pattern blocks.
To understand equivalence.
To develop reasoning skills.

Pg. 10   Hexing Hexagons

Objectives:
To discover all the different ways to make a hexagon.

Answers:
There are 9 ways. If a design can be rotated and/or flipped to produce another one, it is not considered different.

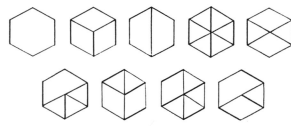

Pg. 11   Take 4

Objectives:
To find solutions using guess and check.
To develop an understanding of area equivalence.

Answers:
Answers may vary.

Explore More:
Yes; yes, except for ⬭.

Top figure: greatest number is 10, least is 3
Middle figure: greatest number is 9, least is 3
Bottom figure: greatest number is 12, least is 4

Pg. 12   Take 6

Objectives:
To find solutions using guess and check.
To develop an understanding of area equivalence.

Answers:
Answers may vary.

Explore More:
Top figure: greatest number is 12, least is 5
Bottom figure: greatest number is 14, least is 6

Pg. 13   One-Color Designs

Objectives:
To learn that a 2 to 1 ratio always exists between the number of triangles and the number of blue rhombi needed to cover equal areas and that a 3 to 2 ratio always exists between blue rhombi and trapezoids.
To practice estimation.

Answers:
Sled : 7 blue rhombi or 14 triangles
Cup : 18 triangles or 9 blue rhombi
Kite : 9 blue rhombi or 6 trapezoids

Explore More:
18; 1 blue rhombus is equivalent to 2 triangles and 1 trapezoid is equivalent to 3 triangles.

Pg. 14   Spaces Zero

Objectives:
To estimate area using different units of measure.
To solve a problem using guess and check.

Explore More:
3; the figure can be covered with 3 hexagons and 6 trapezoids, 2 hexagons and 8 trapezoids, or 1 hexagon and 10 trapezoids.

Pg. 15   Space Creatures

Objectives:
To identify and visualize spatial change.
To make predictions.
To use models to solve problems.

Answers:

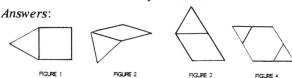

FIGURE 1   FIGURE 2   FIGURE 3   FIGURE 4

Note that only the triangle(s) are moving.

Explore More:
To return to position A, figures 1, 2, and 3 need 4 changes; figure 4 needs 3 changes. After 6 changes, all figures return to position C, except figure 4 which returns to position A. After 8 changes, all figures return to position A, except figure 4 which returns to position C.

Pg. 16   Asteroids

Objectives:
To identify and visualize spatial change.
To make predictions.
To use models to solve problems.

Answers:
If students tape together the blocks needed to make the asteroid, rotations can be done more easily.

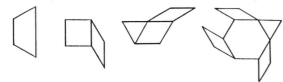

Explore More:
The first, second and third asteroids return to their original positions in 2 minutes. The fourth asteroid returns to its original position in 6 minutes.

Pg. 17 Foursomes

Objectives:
To classify objects.
To solve problems using logic.

Answers:
Label I: All figures in the fence have 4 sides.
Label II: All figures have same perimeter. (If the length of a side of a triangle is 1, the perimeter is 4.)
Label III: All figures have same area. (If the area of the triangle is 1, the area is 4.)

Pg. 18 More Hexagons Or Triangles

Objectives:
To use a table to organize data.
To solve problems by looking for patterns.
To practice mental computation.

Answers:

⬡ x 6 = △

Number of hexagons	Number of triangles
1	6
2	12
3	18
4	24
5	30
6	36
7	42
8	48
9	54
10	60
50	300
100	600
(200-1) 199	1194 (1200-6)

Explore More:

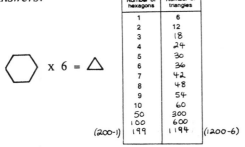 x 7 = △

Number of apples	Number of triangles
1	7
2	14
3	21
4	28
5	35
6	42
7	49
8	56
9	63
10	70
100	700
(200-1) 199	1393 (1400-7)

Pg. 19 Creating Stars

Objectives:
To use a table to organize data.
To solve problems by looking for patterns.
To practice mental computation.

Answers:

✦ x 4 = ▱

✦ x 8 = △

Number of stars	Number of blue rhombi	Number of triangles
1	4	8
2	8	16
3	12	24
4	16	32
5	20	40
6	24	48
7	28	56
8	32	64
9	36	72
10	40	80
50	200	400
49(50-1)	196(200-4)	392(400-8)
200	800	1600

Explore More:

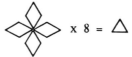 x 3 = ▱

◠ x 9 = △

Number of bridges	Number of trapezoids	Number of triangles
1	3	9
2	6	18
3	9	27
4	12	36
5	15	45
6	18	54
7	21	63
8	24	72
9	27	81
10	30	90
1,000	3,000	9,000
999(1000-1)	2997(3000-3)	8991(9000-9)

Pg. 20 Grab Bag Mystery

Objectives:
To solve problems using guess and check.
To use a table to organize data.

Answers:
3 blue rhombi and 7 trapezoids; 5 blue rhombi and 5 trapezoids

Explore More:
9 blue rhombi and 11 trapezoids

Pg. 21 More Grab Bag Fun

Objectives:
To solve problems using guess and check.
To use a table to organize data.

Answers:
9 trapezoids and 8 hexagons; 72 triangles

Explore More:
5 hexagons and 5 trapezoids

Pg. 22 Building Patterns I

Objectives:
To solve problems by identifying patterns.
To use logic to make predictions.

Answers:
Answers may vary. Possible solutions are:

1. 1 triangle (alternating pattern)
2. 3 rhombi (increasing by one rhombi every other time)
3. 1 rhombus (losing one triangle each time)
4. 9 hexagons (multiplying by 3 each time)
5. 7 squares (adding 2 squares each time) or 9 squares (adding preceding two shapes plus 1 square)

Pg. 23   Building Patterns II

Objectives:
To solve problems by identifying patterns.
To use logic to make predictions.

Answers:
Answers may vary. Possible solutions are:

1. 1 hexagon surrounded by 5 tan rhombi (tan rhombi increasing by the next consecutive odd number)
2. 8 squares (increasing by 2 squares each time) or 10 squares (adding preceding 2 shapes each time) or 12 squares (adding all preceding shapes each time)
3. 1 triangle (decreasing preceding shape by successive unit fractions [½, ⅓, ¼])
4. 16-piece trapezoid (increasing the number of red pieces by adding the next consecutive odd number)

Pg. 24   Triangular Numbers

Objectives:
To introduce triangular numbers.
To use patterns to solve problems.

Answers:
A=1; B=3; C=6; D=10; E=15; F=21

Explore More:
1, 4, 9, 16, 25, ...

Pg. 25   Square Numbers

Objectives:
To introduce square numbers.
To use patterns to solve problems.

Answers:
A=1; B=4; C=9; D=16; E=25; F=36

Explore More:
4; 5; 9; 10; 2500; fiftieth

Pg. 26   Triangular or Square Numbers

Objectives:
To recognize triangular and square numbers.
To use patterns to solve problems.

Answers:
All 3 pattern blocks produce the square number sequence of 1, 4, 9, 16, and 25; larger similar hexagons cannot be made.

Explore More:
The number of orange squares needed for the length always matches the position of the rectangle in the sequence. The width is always one more than the length. The number of orange squares needed equals the length times the width. For example, the 3rd rectangle has 3 squares across, 4 squares down, and a total of 12 squares; the 10th rectangle has 10 squares across, 11 squares down, and a total of 110 orange squares.

Pg. 27   Pattern Block Symmetry

Objectives:
To introduce the concept of symmetry.

Answers:

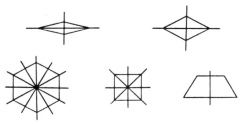

Explore More:
The relative positions of the blocks, not the drawing to scale, is important. Pattern block stickers may be useful.

Pg. 28   Folded Shapes

Objectives:
To identify lines of symmetry.

Answers:

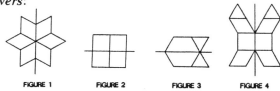

FIGURE 1   FIGURE 2   FIGURE 3   FIGURE 4

Figure 1 has 6; Figure 2 has 4.

Explore More:
The relative positions of the blocks, not the drawing to scale, is important. Pattern block stickers may be useful.

Pg. 29   Simple Symmetry

Objectives:
To identify lines of symmetry.

Answers:
Answers may vary. Have students compare to see how lines of symmetry change when using different blocks.

Pg. 30   Copy Cat

Objectives:
To construct mirror images of pattern block designs.

Answers:

Pg. 31   Scrambled Images

Objectives:
To construct mirror images of complex figures.

Answers:
Answers may vary.

Pg. 32   The Flip Side

Objectives:
To explore the results of flipping a figure.
To generalize to a rule.

Answers:
If students tape together the blocks needed, flipping can be done more easily. Flipping a design an even number of times always results in the original design. Flipping a design an odd number of times always results in the mirror image.

Pg. 33   The Flip Side One More Time

Objectives:
To explore the results of flipping a figure.

Answers:
If students tape together the blocks needed, flipping can be done more easily.

Pg. 34   One Good Turn Deserves Another

Objectives:
To explore rotational symmetry.

Answers:
If students tape together the blocks needed, flipping can be done more easily.

Quarter turn   Half turn   Three-quarter turn

Quarter turn   Half turn   Three-quarter turn

Half turn   Three-quarter turn

Pg. 35   Another Turn

Objectives:
To visualize rotations.

Answers:
If students tape together the blocks needed, flipping can be done more easily.

270° rotation   90° rotation

90°; 180°

Pg. 36   Creative Symmetry I

Objectives:
To use given blocks to construct a design with indicated lines of symmetry.

Answers:
Answers may vary.

Pg. 37   Creative Symmetry II

Objectives:
To use given blocks to construct a design with an indicated number of lines of symmetry.

Answers:
Answers may vary.

Pg. 38   Packages

Objectives:
To explore area and perimeter relationships.

Answers:
5; 5; 7; answers may vary.
10; answers may vary; area doubled; answers may vary.

Explore More:
P=14; area may vary; answers may vary.

Pg. 39   More Packages

Objectives:
To explore area and perimeter relationships.

Answers:
Answers may vary; figures with the same perimeter can have different areas; figures with the same area can have different perimeters.

Pg. 40   Rewrap

Objectives:
To explore area and perimeter relationships.

Answers:
Triangle: 6, 6; blue rhombus: 8, 10; trapezoid: 10, 14; sketches may vary.

Pg. 41   Blocks and Corners

Objectives:
To explore angles and the meaning of congruent angles.

Answers:
A, B, C, and D each have 4 angles; E has 3 angles; F has 6 angles. A, E, and F each have its angles congruent.

Explore More:
The trapezoid and the blue rhombus have angles congruent to those in the hexagon.

Pg. 42   Blocks, Corners and Intersections

Objectives:
To identify angles whose measure is greater than or less than a right angle.

Answers:
4; no

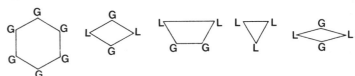

Explore More:

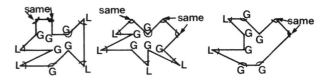

Pg. 43   View From a Right Angle

Objectives:
To identify right, acute, obtuse, and straight angles.

Answers:
Hexagons, blue rhombi, tan rhombi, and trapezoids have obtuse; blue rhombi, tan rhombi, triangles, and

trapezoids have acute; hexagons have only obtuse; triangles have only acute; tan rhombi, blue rhombi, and trapezoids have both; the tan rhombus has both the largest obtuse angle and the smallest acute angle.

Pg. 44   Forming Flowers
Objectives:
To investigate straight angles.

Answers:
12; more; answers may vary

Explore More:
No; sum of the angles are greater than a straight angle.

Pg. 45   Degree Power
Objectives:
To introduce the concept of degrees in angle measurement.

Answers:
90°; 30°; A=60°, B=120°, C=60°, D=120°, E=60°, F=90°, G=150°, H=30°, K=120°

Explore More:
A straight angle is 180°.

Pg. 46   Formulating Formulas
Objectives:
To explore area and perimeter relationships.
To generalize to a formula.
To learn that the dimensions of rectangles with a given area have dimensions that are pairs of factors of that area, i.e., an area of 6 produces 2 possible rectangles—a 1 by 6 and a 2 by 3.

Answers:

Total Area	Rectangle 1		Rectangle 2		Rectangle 3		Rectangle 4	
	Width	Length	Width	Length	Width	Length	Width	Length
6	2	3	1	6				
8	2	4	1	8				
12	3	4	2	6	1	12		

A = 1 x w; the dimensions are the pairs of factors of 20 (1, 20; 2, 10; 4, 5)

Explore More:
1 x 24, 2 x 12, 3 x 8, and 4 x 6

Pg. 47   The Triangle Connection
Objectives:
To develop skills in spatial relationships, i.e., arranging, classifying, rotating, visualizing.

Answers:

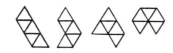

Explore More:
See p. 49.

Pg. 48   Puzzling Pentominoes
Objectives:
To develop skills in spatial relationships, i.e., arranging, classifying, rotating, visualizing.
To reinforce area and perimeter relationships.

Answers:

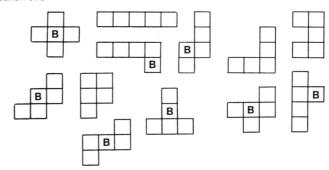

12; they all have a perimeter of 12 except  which has a perimeter of 10.

Explore More:
In the above diagram, the 8 pieces marked with a B.

Pg. 49   The Rhombus Connection
Objectives:
To develop skills in spatial relationships, i.e., arranging, classifying, rotating, visualizing.

Answers:
Authors have found 37 arrangements *so far*. Some are:

Explore More:
The smallest perimeter is 8, the largest is 10.

Area=12
Perimeter=14

Pg. 50   Force Out
Objectives:
To use logical thinking to solve problems.

Explore More:
A force out is inevitable on the 3x3 board, but not on 4x4. A possible solution for a 4x4 is:

1	2	3	4
4	3	2	1
2	1	4	3
3	4	1	2

Pg. 51   Wrapping Figures

Objectives:
To explore making larger, similar figures.
To use patterns to make predictions.

Answers:
Triangle: 4, 16, 49, 100, 169
Square: 9, 25, 49, 81, 121
Blue rhombus: 9, 25, 49, 81, 121

Explore More:
Tan rhombi have the same results as blue rhombi. The trapezoids and hexagons do not form similar figures with wrapping. (A trapezoid can be formed but it is not similar to the original one.)

Pg. 52   Sum Angles

Objectives:
To measure angles.
To learn that the sum of the measure of the angles of a triangle is 180° and that of a quadrilateral is 360°.

Answers:
A=60°, B=60°, C=60°; 180°
D=60°, E=120°, F=60°, G=120°; 360°
K=60°, L=120°, M=120°, N=60°; no, it is 360°.
Brian is adding an extra angle.

360°; yes

Explore More:
Each angle is 120°; the sum is 720.°

Pg. 53   Hidden Wonders

Objectives:
To use visualization to solve problems.
To use guess and check to solve problems.

Answers:
Answers may vary. Some students will need to use the pattern blocks to construct the given figure; others will be able to do the work mentally.

Pg. 54   Hidden Wonders Too

Objectives:
To use visualization to solve problems.
To use guess and check to solve problems.

Answers:
Some students will need to use a large grid and pattern blocks to construct the puzzle piece and fit it physically on the grid; others will be able to do the work mentally.

Pg. 55   Puzzler

Objectives:
To use visualization to solve problems.
To use guess and check to solve problems.

Answers:
Some students will need grid paper and pattern blocks to find correct puzzle pieces; others will be able to do the work mentally.

Omit:

Pg. 56   Double Vision

Objectives:
To perform reflections and draw the results.

Answers:

FIRST REFLECTION   SECOND REFLECTION

FIRST REFLECTION   SECOND REFLECTION

Pg. 57   Clues

Objectives:
To use deductive reasoning.
To use a matrix.

Answers:
Trapezoid (A), triangle (B), hexagon (C)

	⬡	◺	☐	△	▱	◇
Dana	no	no	no	yes	no	no
Vincent	no	yes	no	no	no	no
Sandi	no	no	no	no	yes	no
Bill	no	no	no	no	no	yes